Monographic Journals of the Near East   Afroasiatic Linguistics 1/6 (February 1975)

THE RÔLE OF INDICATOR PARTICLES IN SOMALI

B.W. Andrzejewski

School of Oriental and African Studies
University of London

In Somali there is a number of indicators (phrasal particles) which act as signals of completeness of the sentence and affect the case system and verbal concords. The structures in which they occur have various semantic functions such as the directing of emphasis, making statements and questions, and affirmation and negation.

The formulations presented in this article provide an over-all view of the rôle of indicators and are illustrated by annotated examples, a large proportion of which are drawn from plays, newspaper articles, narratives and proverbs. Although mainly oriented towards data, the article incorporates some of the recent theoretical developments introduced into the Somali field by Robert Hetzron and A.K. Zholkovsky.

CONTENTS

(Roman figures refer to sections)

Section I
INTRODUCTION*

There is a group of particles in Somali which play a very important rôle in the structure of sentences and at the same time have semantic functions which set them apart from all the other word classes in the language. For these particles, which are listed in Section II, I use the term "indicator," first introduced in BE 53,[1] but substantially modified here. To the particles *bǎa, ma⸗*[2] and *waa⸗* which BE 53 describes as indicators I have added six other items, and at the same time I have excluded from the list the particle *la*, which I place in a separate word class and call "impersonal pronoun." In ZH 71 the indicators *bǎa, waa⸗, wǎxa* and *wě̱eyě̱* are referred to as "frazovaya častitsa" ("phrasal particle") a term which has the advantage of stressing their role in sentence structure.

The importance of indicators in Somali, apart from their semantic functions, lies in the fact that with the exception of the cases listed in Section X, every fully formed sentence must have at least one of them. They act thus as signals of completeness of the sentence[3] and their absence, in certain structures, acts as a signal of dependence of a verbal form on the preceding noun or its equivalent. The following examples illustrate this point. In the first sentence the presence of the indicator *bǎa* after *wǐ̱ilkǐi* 'the boy' shows that the sentence is complete, in the second its absence shows that the noun is followed by a dependent verbal clause.

Wǐ̱ilkǐi bǎa yǐmǐ.	'The boy came.'
wǐ̱ilkǐi yǐmǐ	'the boy who came'

In this connection it should be observed that in Somali there are no words corresponding in their function to the English 'who', 'whom' or 'which', as used in relative clauses.

---

*During the researches on which the formulations presented here are based, and which extended over a long period, I received much help from Somali colleagues and friends, too many to mention here by name. I must, however, acknowledge my great debt to Mr. Musa Hajji Ismail Galaal (*Muuse Xaaji Ismaaciil Galaal*). (Note: For biographical and bibliographical information concerning Mr. Musa Galaal see D.R. Dudley and D.M. Lang (ed.), *The Penguin Companion to Literature*, 4 Classical and Byzantine, Oriental and African, Harmondsworth, Penguin Books, 1969, p. 348 and John William Johnson, "Research in Somali folklore," *Research in African Literatures*, 4/1, 1973, pp. 51-61.)

I am very grateful to the members of the Somali Language Committee (*Guddiga Af Soomaaliga*) of the Ministry of Higher Education and Culture, who gave me the opportunity of discussing with them various aspects of Somali grammar, including the impact of indicators on verbal concord, at their sessions in Mogadishu in 1973.

In the preparation and checking of the final draft of this article I received valuable assistance from Mr. Abdisalam Yassin Mohamed (*Cabdisalaan Yaasiin Maxamed*), a young scholar and an accomplished poet, now working on a thesis in the field of Somali literature at the School of Oriental and African Studies, University of London. Mr. J.C.B. Date, a former student at the school, also helped me in the final stages by checking the typescript for errors and inconsistencies and offering some much appreciated suggestions.

Finally I would like to express my thanks to Professor Robert Hetzron, who kindly read the draft of this article and commented on points which required clarification and restatement.

[1]For abbreviated bibliographical references see Section XIV.

[2]The use of the symbol ⸗ is explained later in this section.

[3]This function of indicators receives a great deal of attention in ZH 71: 12 and passim.

All indicators, even though some of them have different, additional semantic functions, carry some degree of emphasis which they impart to certain words or groups of words in their immediate environment. In this respect they perform a function comparable to that of intonation and stress in some languages, such as English for example, where emphasis is expressed by these features.

In Somali, however, comparable accentual features are already used very extensively for other purposes. They act as exponents of

(a) gender and number in nouns (AB 64, AR 34, AN 64a)

(b) case in nouns (AB 64, AN 54, AN 64a, MU 56, ZH 71)

and as integral parts of the inflectional system in nouns (AB 64, AN 64a) and verbs (AB 64, AN 68, AN 69, AN 74a).

The importance of indicators also lies in their role in the concord system, since they act, figuratively speaking, as "selectors" of verbal forms in the sentence. Without reference to them it is impossible to account for the dichotomy between the so-called "extensive" and "restrictive" verbal forms (AN 68). Compare, for example, the following two sentences, where the verbal forms are *yimaaddeen* and *yimi*:

> *Nimánkii wàa yimaaddeen.*

> *Nimánkii bàa yimi.*

Both sentences mean 'The men came', but in the first there is some emphasis on the verb and in the second on the noun. In written English, where stress and intonation are not marked, the nearest translation equivalents of these two sentences would be 'The men did come' and 'It was the men who came', respectively.

The aim of this article is to provide formulations which set out in some detail the salient characteristics of individual indicators within a unified overall framework and to illustrate them with a sizable number of examples. In Sections II – XI, where descriptive formulations are given, the examples consist of very short, simple sentences drawn from the contexts of research sessions with the speakers of the language. Sentences taken from wider contexts, however, are all put together in Section XII and form a large part of this article. The reasons for introducing here this somewhat unusual arrangement are simple. Sentences taken from wider contexts, such as, for example, continuous narratives, often require lengthy annotations to make their form and content completely meaningful to a reader unfamiliar with the language and its culture. Yet such annotations tend to distract the reader and break the continuity of the argument presented. Literal translations might serve as an alternative to annotations, but on account of the vast differences in the word order and rank shifting techniques between English and Somali I have decided to use this device very sparingly. Furthermore some people object to frequent recourse to literal renderings on the grounds that they tend to give a quaint, distorted or even offensive impression of what in the original sounds perfectly normal.

Even though they do not require annotations short sentences used as examples in Sections II – XI present a translation problem. It is a characteristic of Somali that it has no 3sg.m., 3sg.f. and 3pl. forms of the object pronoun (see Section II) and the absence of any word or group of words which could be the object of a transitive verb or a verb with a prepositional particle corresponds, in its semantic function, to the English 'it', 'him', 'her' or 'them', e.g.

> *Wùu arkay.*   'He saw it/him/her/them.'

If a transitive verb takes a double object there could be an even larger number of alternative renderings, e.g.

> *Wùu siiyey.*   'He gave it to him/her/them.'
>   'He "   him to her/them.'
>   'He "   her to him/them.'
>   'He "   them to him/her.'

A similar multiplicity of alternative renderings exists when after an indicator no subject pronoun (see Section II) is used and the verb which follows is in its invariable form i.e. the form which is the same in all persons, e.g.

Mǎ jọogsǎn.   'I/you(sg.)/he/she/we/you(pl.)/they did not stop.'

In order to dispense with the necessity of listing all the alternative translations I have introduced here a convention that when the word "etc." is placed in brackets after a pronoun in the translation two or more renderings are possible but only one is used, e.g.

Mǎ siin.   'He (etc.) did not give it (etc.) to him (etc.).'

The descriptive statements presented in this article apply to the Northern branch of what can be described as Standard (or Common) dialect type. They would require only minor modifications if applied to the other branches of this dialect type or to the Coastal dialect type. For a brief account of the major dialect divisions see AN and LE 64: 37-38 and AN 71: 271-272.

The method of transcription is the same as in AN 64a, except for the following changes:

(a) The symbols ḍ, ħ, ˁ and ˀ are replaced by dh, x, c and ' respectively.

(b) The spelling conventions (i), (iii), (iv) and (v) in AN 64a: 110-113 have been abandoned.

(c) The symbol ¦ is introduced.

The changes (a) and (b) are designed to bring my transcription into almost complete conformity with the Somali national orthography introduced on 21 October 1972 (see AN 74b). After the changes are effected, the only difference between my transcription and the orthography lies in my use of accentual marks, the cedilla and the semicircle over y (y̆). These differences do not imply any criticism of the orthography on my part and result merely from the need of greater precision in linguistic description than in practical communication. The Somali orthography is very well designed as a tool of public and private communication, education and culture and has already contributed substantially to the spectacular progress which Somalia has made in these spheres. In its precision of representing the sounds of the language the Somali orthography compares well with most orthographies in the world including Italian and Polish. It may be appropriate to mention that some of the linguists in the Academy of Culture in Mogadishu are actively engaged in the study of the features represented here by accentual marks and the cedilla (or its absence) in connection with their researches into the lexical resources of the languages.

Since I have abandoned the spelling conventions (i) and (v) in AN 64a: 110-113, I have adopted the general principle implied in the current orthographic practice in Somalia that the transcription represents a flow of speech uninterrupted by any pauses other than those which are indicated by punctuation marks.

Variations in vowel quality are possible in sequences *ay/ey* (very frequent in verbal affixes) and my transcription represents the variant used in the particular utterance at the time when it was written down, from speech or taperecording. This again is done in conformity with the current orthographic practice which leaves a considerable degree of latitude for individual variations. No attempt is made at standardization as set out in the spelling convention (iv) in AN 64a: 112 or as suggested in AR 34: 154.

There are a few words in Somali which, as far as their accentual patterns are concerned, have positional variants (abbreviated here to pos.var.) completely unrelated to any semantic function,[4] e.g.

---

[4]The choice of a particular variant is determined by the accentual patterns, and sometimes also by the grammatical status of the neighbouring words. The rules concerning the distribution of such variants have not been elaborated in detail and require further investigation.

Wâa bêer.	'It is a garden.'
Waa gʒed.	'It is a tree.'

Since such words do not occur in isolation the problem arises as to how they should be marked when discussed in abstraction from any specific context. In my system of representing accentual features (AN 64a: 18-22) absence of any accentual mark is used for one of the accentual units and consequently cannot serve any other purpose. To meet the need of transcribing words without any reference to their accentual features the symbol ! is introduced here. When placed after a particular word it signifies that no accentual features are marked in it.

A detailed account of indicators in Somali requires some preliminary steps. In order to place them within the sentence structure it is first necessary to give definitions of word classes and of certain relevant word groups. This is particularly important since in the literature on Somali there is neither a generally accepted system of classification of such units nor a unified terminology. Unambiguous definitions of word classes are further needed for annotating the sentences which serve as examples of the syntactic environment in which indicators occur.

Section II
WORD CLASSES

In the list given below word classes are defined either by listing their members or by reference to some readily applicable criteria, and references are made to publications in which more extensive information can be found. These references are selective and the reader who wishes to review the whole literature on Somali grammar will find bibliographical guidance in JO 69.

After the name of each class an abbreviation is given which will be used afterwards in formulaic statements and annotations of examples.

DEFINITE ARTICLE OF THE GENERAL TYPE (DEF.ART.GEN.)

ka, ta

> AN 61: 81, 97-98; AN 64a: 118-120.
> The form beginning with *k-* is masculine and the one beginning with *t-* is feminine; the same applies to all the other articles and definitives listed below. For information concerning gender in Somali see AB 64 and BE 53.

DEFINITE ARTICLE OF THE REMOTE TYPE (DEF.ART.REM.)

kii, tii

> The same references as above.

DEMONSTRATIVE (DEM.)

kán, tán 'this'; *káas (káa), táas (táa)* 'that' (sometimes also 'this'); *kéer, téer* 'that'; *kóo, tóo* 'that'.

Note that *kéer, téer* and *kóo, tóo* are obsolescent and most speakers have doubts about their exact meaning, even though they recognize their deictic function.

> AN 64a: 118-120; BE 53: 18-19.

POSSESSIVE DEFINITIVE (POSS.DEF.)

kay⌐, tay⌐ 'my'; *kaa⌐, taa⌐* 'your' (sg.); *kͬis⌐, tͬis⌐* 'his'; *kͬed⌐, tͬed⌐* 'her'; *kayo⌐, tayo⌐* 'our' (excl.); *kͬen⌐, tͬen⌐* 'our' (incl.); *kͬin⌐, tͬin⌐* 'your' (pl.); *kͬod⌐, tͬod⌐* 'their'.

> AN 64a: 119-120; BE 53: 69-70.

INTERROGATIVE DEFINITIVE (INTER.DEF.)

kͬe (kͬee), tͬe (tͬee) 'which?'

> AN 64a: 120; BE 53: 54.

INDEFINITE ARTICLE (INDEF.ART.)

ku, tu
The indefinite article appears to be obsolescent. I have found examples of it in only one type of phrase: *ku kalê* and *tu kalê*, both meaning 'another one' (but with a difference in gender). This article should not be confused with the B Case (Subject Case) forms of *ka, ta* (def.art.gen.) as shown in AN 64a: 119 and BE 53: 13.

NOUN (N.)

> The main identifying criteria of this word class are:

> (a) Its members are capable of combining with at least one of the following classes: def.art.gen., def.art.rem., dem.,poss.def. or inter.def.; such combinations are characterized by special types of phonological junctions (AN 64a: 121-124).

> (b) It is an open word class, i.e. its membership is capable of expansion at any time by borrowing or innovation. By this definition the following word classes are not considered as nouns, even though they fulfill the conditions given in (a) above: poss.def., card.num., appr.num., unsp.num., subs.pron. and rec. pron.

By the application of the above criteria this word class includes proper names (which for practical, not theoretical, reasons were not covered in AN 64a) and various words denoting time, space and manner, such as *càawa* 'tonight', *àg* 'near', 'vicinity', or *sáhal* 'easily', 'ease'.

When an individual noun is referred to in the annotation of an example in this article it is first given in the form it has when it occurs in isolation i.e. in its representative form (lexical entry form); this form is followed by an explanation of the form it has in the particular text by reference to its setting, configuration and case (see Section V). The abbreviations m. and f. mean "masculine" and "feminine" respectively. The distinction between plural (pl.) and sub-plural (sub-pl.) is based on different types of concord with verbal forms but does not involve any differentiation of meaning. Collective (coll.) forms are those which are plural in meaning but do not have any formal exponents characteristic of the plural or sub-plural forms.

> AN 64a; BE 53, especially 72-73 and 77-78; ZH 66: 158-159.
> On verbal concord:[5] AN 64a: 28-29 and HE 72: 259-261.

---

[5]The table of concords given in AN 64a: 28 requires an adjustment. Below the entry "plural" another entry should be inserted: masculine, sub-plural; the agreeing verbal forms are the same as in the entry for "plural" i.e. 3pl. in both columns. See also Section VII (e) and (f) of this article.

ADVERBIAL NOUN I (ADV.N.I)

horê (horêy) 'forward', 'before'; *sarê* 'up'

This class consists only of two members which occupy positions in the sentence comparable to nouns denoting space or time, but do not conform to the first of the criteria set down for nouns. They are always followed by the prep.ptc. *u*‌⁻ and a verb.

AB 64: 110.

ADVERBIAL NOUN II (ADV.N.II)

ǧad   'much', 'very', 'thoroughly'

This word occupies positions in the sentence which are comparable to those of nouns, though not all of them. It does not conform to the first of the criteria set down for nouns. The adv.n.II is often, though not always, followed by the prep.ptc. *u*‌⁻ and a verb.

AB 64: 3, where 'muchness' is given as the first meaning.

CARDINAL NUMERAL (CARD.NUM.)

The members of this class form the series *kǫw* 'one', *lâba* 'two', *sâddex* 'three', *áfar* 'four', *shăn* 'five' etc. Note that *mîd* 'one' which occurs in certain contexts (BE 53: 48) is also included in this class.

BE 53: 48-49.

APPROXIMATING NUMERAL (APPR.NUM.)

This class is composed of words which could be regarded as combinations of roots present in cardinal numerals and the suffix *-eeyo*, e.g. *tobanêeyo* 'approximately ten', cf. *tobăn* 'ten'; *afartanêeyo* 'approximately forty', cf. *afártan* 'forty'.

UNSPECIFIED NUMERAL (UNSP.NUM.)

dhăwr 'several'

Note that nouns which occur with this word have the same "post-numeral" forms as when they occur with cardinal or approximating numerals (AN 64a: 65-66).

SUBSTANTIVE PRONOUN (SUBS.PRON.)

ani‌⁻ 'I', 'me'; *adi*‌⁻ 'you'(sg.); *isa*‌⁻ 'he', 'him'; *iya*‌⁻ 'she', 'her'; *anna*‌⁻ 'we', 'us'(excl.); *inna*‌⁻ 'we', 'us'(incl.); *idin*‌⁻ 'you'(pl.); *iya*‌⁻ 'they', 'them'.

AN 61; BE 53: 30 and 40; ZH 71: 44.

Subs.pron. occur very frequently as components of the nom.aggr.I and sometimes as components of the nom.aggr.II (see Section III). When *ani* and *adi* are immediately followed by the conj. *iyo*‌⁻, *na*‌⁻, *oo*‌⁻ or *se*‌⁻ they combine into the following forms: *aniyo*‌⁻, *anna*‌⁻, *anoo*‌⁻, *anse*‌⁻, *adiyo*‌⁻, *adna*‌⁻, *adoo*‌⁻, *adse*‌⁻; when *isa* combines with the conj. *na*‌⁻ the combined form is *isna*‌⁻.

Note that only *ani* and *adi* can be immediately followed by the ind. *băa*, and this accounts for a certain asymmetry in Table I in Section IV.

INTERROGATIVE WORD, TYPE I (INTER.W.I)

This class is composed of words which are combinations of nouns or substantive pronouns and the suffix -ma, e.g. *gŏorma* 'what time?' cf. *gŏor* (n.f.) 'time'; *mĕelma* 'which place?', c.f. *mĕel* (n.f.) 'place'; *idínma* 'which of you?', cf. *idin*⸎ (subs.pron.) 'you'(pl.).

Note that such combinations do not conform to criterion (a) which is applied to nouns and they are consequently treated as a separate class.

INTERROGATIVE WORD, TYPE II (INTER.W.II)

maxáy 'what?'

Note that the form *maxàa* given in BE 53: 55-56 is a contraction of *maxáy + bàa* (MU 56: 22).

INTERROGATIVE WORD, TYPE III (INTER.W.III)

kúma, túma, kuwáma   'who?', 'whom?' (sg.m., sg.f. and pl. respectively)

Tentatively these words may be regarded as combinations of the indef.art. and the same suffix as in inter.w.I.

INTERROGATIVE WORD, TYPE IV (INTER.W.IV)

yaa⸎   'who?', 'whom?'

        BE 53:55.

INTERROGATIVE WORD, TYPE V (INTER.W.V)

ayŏ   'who?'

INTERROGATIVE WORD, TYPE VI (INTER.W.VI)

ímisa (ímmisa)   'how many?', 'how much?'

        BE 53: 49.

INTERROGATIVE WORD, TYPE VII (INTER.W.VII)

mĝe (mĝeyey) 'where is he (it)?', *mĕeday* 'where is she (it)?', *meeyĕ* 'where are they?'

These forms can be assumed to contain verbal components, possibly related to some forms of the verb *yghay* 'to be' (AN 69: 48-50).

        BE 53: 54.

RECIPROCAL PRONOUN (REC.PRON.)

is   'each other', 'one another', 'self'

Note that in certain contexts this word can combine with forms of the poss.def., e.g. *iskáa* 'yourself'.

SUBJECT PRONOUN (SUBJ.PRON.)

aan 'I'; *aad* (*aa*) 'you'(sg.); *uu* 'he'; *ay* 'she'; *aannu* (*aan*) 'we'(excl.); *aynu* 'we'(incl.); *aad* (*aydin*, *aa*) 'you'(pl.); *ay* 'they'.

Note that the accentual patterns of the members of this class shown here apply to all contexts, except those discussed in HE 65: 125; paragraph (e) (ii) A.

> AN 61: 93, where the term "preverbal subject pronoun" is used; BE 53: 30 (column 2).

IMPERSONAL PRONOUN (IMPERS.PRON.)

la   'someone', 'one', 'people', 'they', 'an unspecified person'.

> AN 60: 103; BE 53: 99, where the term "impersonal indicator" is used.

OBJECT PRONOUN, TYPE I (OBJ.PRON.I)

i   'me'; *ku* 'you'(sg.); *na* 'us'(excl.); *ina* (*inna*) 'us'(excl.); *idin* 'you'(pl.)

Note that in this series the 3sg.m., 3sg.f. and 3pl. do not exist.

> AN 60: 103; BE 53: 40 (column 2).

OBJECT PRONOUN, TYPE II (OBJ.PRON.II)

kay⁻ 'me'; *kaa*⁻ 'you'(sg.); *kayo*⁻ 'us'(excl.); *keen*⁻ 'us'(incl.); *kiin*⁻ 'you'(pl.)

A member of this class can occur only when it is preceded by an obj.pron.I or the rec.pron.

> MU 56: 125 (Note 237); ZH 66: 159 (column 8), where the relative position of these pronouns in preverbal sequences is given.

ATTRIBUTIVES (ATTR.)

dambe 'which is behind'; *dhexe* 'which is in the middle'; *hoose* 'which is below'; *hore* 'which is before', 'which is first'; *kale* 'other'; *kasta* 'every'; *kore* 'which is at the top', 'which is above'; *sare* the same meaning as *kore*; *shishe* 'which is beyond', 'which is on the other side'; *soke* 'which is on this side'; *walba* (*walba*) 'each'.

Note that *walba* (*walba*) may be regarded as a compound of *wal* and the distr.ptc. *ba*⁻, described later in this section, or even as a phrase composed of these two words.

> AN 64a: 126-127; BE 53: 84-85, where the term "local attributive" is used.

ORDINAL NUMERALS (ORD.NUM.)

The members of this class form the series *koobaad* 'first'; *labaad* 'second'; *saddexaad* 'third'; *afraad* 'fourth'; *shanaad* 'fifth' etc.

> BE 53: 75.

VERB (V.)

The members of this class are characterized by having formal exponents of pronominal reference, time reference and reference to the mode of action or state which they denote. Verbs are divided into three groups: weak, hybrid and strong. Weak and hybrid verbs are described in

AN 68[6] and AN 69 respectively, where they are subdivided into root extension classes. There are only five strong verbs (identified by the code letters STR): the verb *yahay* 'to be' (AN 69: 48-50) and four verbs with vocalic mutation (AN 74a).

Note that in BE 53 a different classification is used and it corresponds with mine in the following way:

> weak verbs = Conjugations 1, 1A-C, 2, 3, 3A-C
>
> hybrid verbs = all adjectives except *ah* (BE 53: 76-78) and Conjugation 4 (Attributive Verbs) (BE 53: 80-83)
>
> strong verbs = Irregular Verbs (BE 53: 32) and the verb *yahay* 'to be', which is assigned to Conjugation 4, except for its *ah* form which is treated as an adjective (BE 53: 80-83 and 78)

When individual verbs are referred to in annotations of examples they are given in their representative forms (i.e. lexical entry forms) as defined in AN 68, AN 69 and AN 74a: 2sg.imper. for all weak verbs, pres.res. for all hybrid verbs, 3sg.m.past gen.ext. for all strong verbs except *yahay* 'to be' which is given in the 3sg.m.pres. ext. In such annotations every weak or hybrid verb is provided with capital code letters representing its root extension class according to the classification given in AN 68 and AN 69; the sign † after such code letters shows that the verb belongs to the hybrid group and its absence that it belongs to the weak group.

INDICATOR (IND.)

I. *bàa* (*ayàa, yàa*); II. *ha⸱*; III. *miyàa*; IV. *ma⸱*; V. *soo⸱* (*sow⸱, show⸱*);
VI. *waa⸱*; VII. *wàxa* (*waxàa*); VIII. *weeyè⸱* (*weeyàan⸱*); IX. *yaan⸱* (*yaa⸱*).

   I.   AN 61: 88; AN 64a: 46-47, 128, 139-140; AN 68: 4; BE 53: 25-27, 29, 34-35; HE 65; MU 56: 22; ZH 71: 12-22 and passim.

  II.   BE 53: 23-24, 93; MU 56: 74.

 III.   AN 61: 88; AN 64a: 47.

  IV.   BE 53: 56, 66-68.

   V.   BE 53: 111; MU 56: 66 (Note 1/12B, a and c).
        This ind. is regarded here as a different word from *sow⸱* (*show⸱*), which introduces an element of suspense or surprise into the narrative and is assigned to class r.i. described later in this section. See MU 56: 66, Note 12B (b).

  VI.   AN 64a: 138-139; BE 53: 25-28; ZH 71: 12-22 and passim.

 VII.   AN 64a: 140-141; AN 68: 44; BE 53: 60; HE 74b; ZH 71: 194-197 and passim.

VIII.   BE 53: 83-84; ZH 71: 12-22 and passim.
        This ind. is regarded as a different word from *weeyè*, a word which is used merely as a signal that one is paying attention to what is said, assigned to class r.i.

  IX.   BE 53: 93-94.

Since indicators are "phrasal particles" it is very difficult to provide them with succinct translations. Their semantic functions can be inferred from the formulations provided in Sections VI and VII.

---

[6] In this publication the following emendations should be made: P.11, *dhisanayaa* > *dhisánayaa*, P.12, *dhisáyaa* > *dhísayaa*, *dïidayaa* > *dïidayaa*, *maqashïinayn* > *maqashïináyn*.

PREPOSITIONAL PARTICLE (PREP.PTC.)

*u*ᵈ 'to', 'for'; *ku*ᵈ 'in', 'with' (expressing instrumentality); *ka*ᵈ 'from'; *la*ᵈ 'together with'.

   AN 60; BE 53: 21-22, where the term "prepositions" is used; ZH 66.

ADVERBIAL PARTICLE (ADV.PTC.)

kala 'apart'; *wada* 'together', 'altogether'; *sóo* 'towards what is regarded as the centre of attention'; *sii* 'away from what is regarded as the centre of attention.

   AN 60: 101; BE 53: 22, where *sóo* and *sii* are referred to as "adverbs"; ZH 66: 158-159.

DISTRIBUTIVE PARTICLE (DISTR.PTC.)

*ba*ᵈ 'each', 'whatever', 'whoever', 'all', 'altogether'

   BE 53: 75; MJ 56: 67-68 (Notes 1/13-14 and 1/14A).

DECLARATIVE PARTICLE (DECL.PTC.)

in 'that' as in *waan ǧgahay inuu yimi* 'I know that he came' or *wâxaan dǧonayaa inaan ku arkó* 'I want to see you' (lit. 'I want that I see you').

   BE 53: 92; MJ 56: 65, Note 10(d).
   Note that this particle is treated here as a different word from *in*(n.f.) 'amount', 'period of time', 'group', the full range of meanings of which is given in MJ 56: 65, Note 10(a-c) and MJ 56: 67, Note 13-14.

CONCESSIVE PARTICLE (CCV.PTC.)

wḡlow 'although', 'even though' (Arabic: *wa law*).

TERMINAL PARTICLE (TERM.PTC.)

*ilaa*ᵈ 'as far as', 'as far back as', 'until', 'since' (Arabic *ilā*).

   BE 53: 20, where it is referred to as "preposition."

NEGATION PARTICLE (NEG.PTC.)

*aan*ᵈ

   BE 53: 96; MJ 56: 68, Note 15B.

CONJUNCTION (CONJ.)

*amma*ᵈ (*ama*ᵈ) 'or'; *ee*ᵈ (*e*ᵈ) 'and', 'but'; *iyo*ᵈ 'and'; *na*ᵈ 'and', 'but'; *oo*ᵈ 'and', 'while'; *se*ᵈ 'but', 'yet'; *toona*ᵈ 'neither'.

   BE 53: 42-43, 110, where the term "coordinate" is used; MJ 56: 77, Note 7A.

RESIDUAL ITEM (R.I.)

This class consists of words which do not belong to any of the classes given above.

EXCURSUS ON *wáxa*

In the list of word classes given above *wáxa* is classified as an indicator and this presents
a substantial departure from my previous treatment of this word (AN 64a: 140-141 and AN 68:
44). There I regarded the constructions with *wáxa* as verbless sentences composed of two
parts: the inceptive part in which *wáxa* was treated as the noun *wăx* 'thing', 'things',
'person', 'persons' + the def.art.gen.m. followed by a dependent verbal clause, and the
sequel part consisting of a noun or its equivalent. The juxtaposition of the two parts was
then said to imply the meaning corresponding to the English 'is', 'are', and the whole
sentence was regarded as verbless i.e. containing no main verb, e.g.

Wáxay dǧonaysaa dhár.	'What she wants [is] clothes.'
	Note that *wáxay = wáxa* and *ay* 'she'.
Wáxa nalá jǫogtá gabádh.	'The person who is staying with us [is] a girl.'

In sentences of this kind I now regard *wáxa* as an indicator comparable with *bàa* and not as a
noun + def.art.gen., and the verbal forms involved as main and not dependent verbs. The
revised approach makes it necessary to restate the distribution rules given in AN 68: 44, and
such a restatement is provided in Section VII of this article. It must be pointed out that
the old and the new rules are mutually convertible on account of the complete homonymy
between the dependent and the main verbal forms in question. The homonymous paradigms are
given side by side in the table below:

DEPENDENT POSITIVE	MAIN POSITIVE
All divergent B paradigms:	All extensive paradigms
All convergent A paradigms:	All restrictive paradigms
DEPENDENT NEGATIVE	MAIN NEGATIVE
All invariable A paradigms:	All invariable paradigms

In view of the new approach to the type of sentences under discussion I propose to introduce
a new term and call them "heralding sentences." The choice of the term is suggested by the
fact that the indicator *wáxa* places emphasis on the noun or its equivalent which comes later
in the sentence, thus heralding, as it were, its arrival (see Section VI).

It must be observed that the noun *wăx* (+ the def.art.gen.) frequently occurs as the headword
of a nominal cluster containing a dependent clause which may outwardly resemble the first
part of a heralding sentence, e.g.

Wáxay dǧonaysó síi!	'Give her the thing which she wants!'

No ambiguity can occur, however, since such nominal clusters follow the same rules as any
other nominal clusters and function as noun equivalents in the sentence. Even in cases which
give the impression of similarity heralding sentences are always differentiated formally
from other sentences. Compare, for example, the following sentences:

Wáxay tidhi garán màayó.	'She said, "I do not know it (etc.)."'
Wáxay tidhí garán màayó.	'I (etc.) do not know what she said.'
	(Lit. 'I do not know the thing which she said.')

The change in my treatment of *wáxa* in heralding sentences is due to the new formulations
presented in ZH 71 which a mathematician would describe as an elegant solution to a very
complex problem. The formulations in ZH 71 fit the general framework of Somali sentence
patterns much better, firstly by treating *wáxa* as a phrasal particle (= indicator in my
terminology) and secondly by eliminating the following apparent anomalies inherent in the
previous treatment:

(a) The asymmetry in the use of verbal forms A and B, in the rules provided in AN 68: 44.

(b) The fact that in heralding sentences *wáxa*, if treated as a noun + def.art.gen., cannot occur in its plural form (*waxyaalŏ, waxyaabŏ*) or combine with def.art.rem. or dem.

(c) The characteristics of concord in such sentences as: *Wáxa timí gabádh.* 'A girl came'. The concord here is between *timí* 'came' (3sg.f.) and *gabádh* 'girl', and not between *wáxa* and *timí* , since the noun *wáx* is masculine and would require the verbal form *yimí* 'came' (3sg.m.).

While studying the formulations in ZH 71 I reexamined the relationship between heralding sentences and corresponding sentences which contain the indicator *bàa*, and came to conclusions which are entirely in favour of regarding *wáxa* as comparable with *bàa*. All heralding sentences can be derived from statement sentences (see Section VI and VII) containing *bàa* and a main verb, by the application of a very simple rule: 'Replace *bàa* by *wáxa* and transpose the noun or its equivalent[7] which immediately precedes *bàa* to the end of the sentence,' e.g.

> *Dhár bày dǧonaysaa.*
>
> *Wáxay dǧonaysaa dhár.*

Both sentences have the same meaning: 'She wants clothes.' The only difference between them is that the emphasis on *dhár* 'clothes' is indicated in the first sentence by *bàa* (as *bày = bàa + ay*) and in the second sentence by *wáxa* (as *wáxay = wáxa + ay*). Note that the first of these sentences could be regarded as a type of cleft sentence (HE 65: 130) and translated as 'It is clothes that she wants.' The second sentence, on the other hand, could be regarded as a sentence of cataphoric type, described in HE 74b, in which case the nearest English equivalent in translation would be 'What she wants is clothes'. Although in the present article I have not adopted this interpretation I am fully aware that it constitutes a valid alternative. HE 74b is an important paper, highly relevant to the study of heralding sentences in Somali. In this work which covers a large number of languages and aims at establishing universals, Hetzron views the Somali sentences under discussion as examples of Presentative Movement, a phenomenon which accounts for the occurrence of the focused element in the final position in the sentence. Since I have at my disposal only the preliminary version of this paper I leave my comments till the next opportunity of discussing it in detail. I entirely agree, however, with Hetzron's treatment of heralding sentences in Somali as structures which exemplify "presentativeness." He is right when, speaking about them, he says, "It is the only way in Somali to bring the presentative element to the end of the sentence." In fact, it seems that the main function of these sentences is to postpone the particularly important element till the end, using the first part of the sentence as a device for heralding that element.

---

[7]There are, however, some restrictions as to the nature of such a noun-equivalent. It can consist only of one of the items listed as N4 or N7 in Table I, Section IV, and if that item is a nominal cluster or a para-nominal cluster II (see Section III) there is a further restriction. A dependent verbal form which occurs in such clusters before *bàa* can have either form A or B, if the B form ends in *-aa* or *-aan*, the choice being optional. The derivational rule given here operates only if A form occurs. A similar choice between forms A and B in dependent verbal forms is also possible in para-nominal clusters I and the same restriction applies if the cluster conveys factual information. When it refers to an intention, wish, purpose or obligation, there is a similar optional choice but it is unrelated to the presence or absence of *bàa* and does not restrict the operation of the rule.

Section III

AGGREGATES, CLUSTERS AND QUOTED PIECES

In addition to word classes it is necessary for the description of structures in which indicators occur to establish units which will be termed here nominal aggregates, nominal clusters, para-nominal clusters and quoted pieces.

The term nominal aggregate (nom.aggr.)[8] is applied to the combinations of word classes given below:

	def.art.gen.		def.art.gen.	+ dem.	*kǎn, tǎn*
n.	def.art.rem.		poss.def.	+ def.art.gen.
card.num.	dem.	OR +	poss.def.	+ def.art.rem.
appr.num.	+	poss.def.		poss.def.	+ dem.
unsp.num.	inter.def.		poss.def.	+ inter.def.

	def.art.gen.
subs.pron.	def.art.rem.
poss.def. +	dem.
	inter.def.

rec.pron. +	poss.def.

These combinations are characterized by special types of phonological junctions, described in detail in AN 64a: 119-124 and 126; they form units into which no other words can be inserted. The first component in each of these combinations acts as its headword in the sense that the other components are dependent on it. It should be noted that only the headword is capable of concord with a verbal form.

Nominal aggregates are divided into those which do not contain an inter.def. and those which do. They will be referred to as nom.aggr.I and nom.aggr.II respectively.

The concept of nominal cluster (abbreviated to nom.cl.) is explained in some detail in AN 64a: 40-45 and only a brief description will be given here. It is a syntactic unit, which acts as a "noun substitute" and consists of one of the constructions given below:

    (a) a headword accompanied by a word or group of words dependent on it;

    (b) words or syntactic units linked to one another by the conjunction *iyo*⸗ 'and'.

In a construction of type (a) the headword can be one of the following: def.art.gen., def.art.rem., dem., indef.art., n., card.num., appr.num., unsp.num., subs.pron. or nom.aggr.I; the dependent word or group of words can be: n., attr., ord.num., nom.aggr.I, nom.cl. or a dependent verbal clause.

In a construction of type (b) the following words or groups of words can be involved: def. art.rem., dem., n., card.num., appr.num., unsp.num., subs.pron., nom.aggr.I and II, nom.cl., para-nom.cl.I and II or quot.p. Note that the last three of these items are described later in this section.

---

[8]The term "nom.aggr." corresponds to the term "defined noun" in BE 53 and AN 64a.

In nominal clusters which contain a dependent clause the headword is often a noun which denotes time, manner or condition. When this happens the nominal cluster is comparable, from the point of view of the meaning it conveys, to adverbial clauses in English, e.g.

mărkuu arkăy	'when he came', lit. '[at] the time when he came'
ĭntuu jgogăy	'while he stayed', lit. '[during] the time when he stayed'
sĭduu ŭ helăy	'how he found it', lit. 'the manner in which he found it'
haddŭu yĭmaaddŏ	'if he comes', lit. '[under] the condition that he comes'

By para-nominal cluster (abbreviated to para-nom.cl.) is understood here a construction identical with the type of nominal cluster which contains a dependent verb clause, except that its headword is a particle. Para-nominal clusters are divided into three types:

Type I, where the headword is the decl.ptc. *ĭn* 'that'.

Type II, where the headword is the term.ptc. *iłăa* 'until', 'since'.

Type III, where the headword is the ccv.ptc. *wĕlow* 'although', 'even though'.

Frequently a piece of direct speech consisting of a word or a group of words forms an integral part of a Somali sentence, e.g.

Hăa băy yĭdhaahdeen.	'They said "yes".'
Shăłay băy keeneen bŭu yĭdhi.	'"They brought it yesterday," he said.'

In both sentences the direct speech occupies a position comparable to that of a n., nom.aggr.I or II, or nom.cl. For this reason it is treated here as a syntactic unit and will be referred to as "quoted piece" (abbreviated to quot.p.).

The internal structure of this unit is independent of the structure of the sentence within which it occurs and can, theoretically, be of any length.

Section IV

NOMINAL AND VERBAL UNITS

In addition to the preliminary steps towards the description of the roles of indicators taken in Sections II and III two substitution series are established here, which will be referred to as N and V units.

N units consist of a series of items indicated by the sign + in the columns of Table I below. The figures at the top of each column give the serial number of each unit. These units will be used in formulations describing structures, where they will represent ANY ONE (but only one) item within each series. Thus for example N2 means: "any one of the following: dem., n., card.num., appr.num., unsp.num., subj.pron., impers.pron., nom.aggr.I, nom.cl."

V units consist of substitutuion series of verbal forms listed in Table II below. Infinitives + auxiliary verbs are treated here as single units for the purposes of this classification and in such cases the designation of the unit is regarded as determined by the form of the auxiliary verb and not by that of the infinitive. Note, however, that the infinitive can occur by itself, without an auxiliary verb, as a selfstanding unit, usually with future time reference.

The names of verbal paradigms are the same as in AN 68: 2-3 and AN 69: 54-55 and the abbreviations used are: [continued on p. 19]

TABLE I

	N units										
	1	2	3	4	5	6	7	8	9	10	11
dem.	+	+	+	+	+	+	+	+	+	+	+
inter.def.	+				+			+			+
n.	+	+	+	+	+	+	+	+	+	+	+
adv.n.I and II	+		+								
card.num.	+	+	+	+	+	+	+	+	+	+	+
appr.num.	+	+	+	+	+	+	+	+	+	+	+
unsp.num.	+	+	+	+	+	+	+	+	+	+	+
1sg. & 2sg. subs.pron.[9]	+		+		+	+			+		
inter.w.I	+				+			+			
inter.w.II	+				+			+			
inter.w.III	+				+			+			+
inter.w.IV											+
inter.w.V								+			
inter.w.VI	+				+			+			+
subj.pron.		+									
impers.pron.		+									
nom.aggr.I	+	+	+	+	+	+	+	+	+	+	+
nom.aggr.II	+				+			+			+
nom.cl.	+	+	+	+	+	+	+	+	+	+	+
para-nom.cl.I	+		+	+	+	+	+	+	+	+	+
para-nom.cl.II	+		+	+							
para-nom.cl.III	+		+								
quot.p.	+		+	+	+	+	+	+			+

---

[9]Note, however, that all persons of the subs.pron. occur frequently as components of the nom.aggr.I and sometimes as components of the nom.aggr.II (see AN 61: 81-82 and 98).

TABLE II

	V units									
	1	2	3	4	5	6	7	8	9	0
imper.										+
pres.gen.ext.	+									
pres.cnt.ext.	+									
pres.gen.res.			+							
pres.cnt.res.			+							
past gen.ext.	+									
past cnt.ext.	+									
past gen.res.			+							
past cnt.res.			+							
past indep.										+
1sg, 2sg., 1pl. & 2pl.optat.										+
3sg.m., 3sg.f. & 3pl.optat.								+		
rhet.				+						
poten.						+				
inf.	+		+							
neg.imper.									+	
neg.pres.gen.					+					
neg.pres.cnt.var.					+					
neg.pres.-past gen.		+			+					
neg.pres.cnt.inv.		+			+					
neg.past cnt.		+			+					
neg.opt.							+			
neg.cond.					+					

(i) appears at the left margin beside the 3sg.m./3sg.f. & 3pl.optat. row.

TABLE II (continued)

(ii)		V units									
		1	2	3	4	5	6	7	8	9	0
	pres.ext.	+									
	past ext.	+									
	pres.res.			+							
	past res.			+							
	pres.comp.										+
	past comp.										+
	pres.exclam.										+
	past exclam.										+
	neg.pres.					+					
	neg.pres.-past		+			+					

(continued from page 16)

cnt.	continuous		inv.	invariable
comp.	comparative		neg.	negative
cond.	conditional		optat.	optative
exclam.	exclamatory		poten.	potential
ext.	extensive		pres.	present
gen.	general		res.	restrictive
imper.	imperative		rhet.	rhetorical
indep.	independent		var.	variable
inf.	infinitive			

It might be of interest to note that the terms "extensive" and "restrictive" do not refer to any specific semantic function of the verbal forms in question. They serve merely as labels for different verbal paradigms whose selection is determined by the position of certain indicators in the sentence, as will be seen from the formulations provided in Section VII. For a historical account of the dichotomy between extensive and restrictive paradigms in Somali and other Cushitic languages see HE 74a.

Like N units, V units are indicated by the sign + in the table below and will be used in describing structures, where they will represent ANY ONE unit of each series. Thus for example V3 means: "any one (but ONLY ONE) verbal form which belongs to any of the following paradigms: pres.gen.res., pres.cnt.res., past gen.res., past cnt.res., inf., pres.res., past res."

Group (i) refers to all weak verbs and all strong verbs except for *yqhay* 'to be'. Group (ii) refers to all hybrid verbs and the verb *yqhay*, but it should be noted that this verb does not occur in pres.comp., past comp., pres.exclam. and past exclam.

Section V

INDICATORS AND THE CASE SYSTEM

As demonstrated in AN 64a there is a two term case system in Somali nouns. Compare, for example, *àaʀ* 'a male lion' (case A) and *aaʀ*, the same meaning, (case B) in the two sentences below. For the significance of placing words or groups of words between exclamation marks, see the part of Section VI which deals with emphasis.

> *Àaʀ mâ qabtay?*
> '(!)Did(!) he (!)catch(!) a male lion?'
>
> *Aaʀ mâ qabtay?*
> '(!)Did(!) a male lion (!)catch(!) him (etc.)?'

Case differentiation of this kind does not occur, however, in certain contexts, namely:

   (i)   when the noun is emphasized and is preceded by ind. *waa-* or *wâxa* (*waxâa*) or followed by *wẹeyê* (*wẹeyàan*),

   (ii) when the noun is emphasized and is followed by ind. *bâa* (*ayâa, yâa*) or *miyâa* and,

   (iii) when the noun is followed by an item dependent on it or is linked by a conjunction to an item parallel to it (i.e. an item not dependent on it).

Examples:

   (i)   *Wûxuu* (= *wâxa uu*) *qabtay àaʀ.*
         'He caught (!)a male lion(!).'

         Wâxa qabtáy àaʀ.
         '(!)A male lion(!) caught him (etc.).'

   (ii) *Àaʀ bâa wʒil qabtay.*
         'A boy caught (!)a male lion(!).'

         Àaʀ bâa wʒil qabtáy.
         '(!)A male lion(!) caught a boy.'

   (iii) *Àaʀ wẹyn mâ qabtay?*
         '(!)Did(!) he (!)catch(!) a big male lion?' (Lit. 'a lion which is big')

         Àaʀ wẹyni mâ qabtay?
         '(!)Did(!) a big male lion (!)catch(!) him (etc.)?'

         Àaʀ iyo qôol mâ qabteen?
         '(!)Did(!) they (!)catch(!) a male lion and a lioness?'

         Àaʀ iyo qooli mâ qabteen?
         '(!)Did(!) a male lion and a lioness (!)catch(!) him (etc.)?'

Each type of context which determines the presence or absence of case differentiation in a noun is referred to as its configuration, a term introduced in AN 64a: 45-48. The contexts described in (i), (ii), and (iii) above are called neutral,[10] closed and concatenated configurations respectively and the context in which case differentiation can occur is called open configuration.

---

[10]In view of what has been said in Section II concerning sentences containing the ind. *wâxa*, the wording of the definition of neutral configuration in AN 64a: 45-46 should be changed by substituting "a verbless sentence of *wax*-type" by "a heralding sentence." Note that "sequel part" corresponds to N4 and N7 in the formulations given in Table III in Section VII. In addition this definition should be enlarged by including in it the position before *wẹeyê* or after *wâxa wẹeyê* (see Table III, Section VII).

A noun in concatenated configuration forms, *ipso facto*, part of a nominal cluster. If such a nominal cluster taken as a unit occurs in open configuration, case differentiation is displaced, as it were, from the noun to the marker of the nominal cluster. By marker is understood here the last component of the nominal cluster which is directly dependent on its headword (or one of its headwords) or is the last headword (if there are more than one). How this displacement operates can be shown by reference to two pairs of examples already cited, in which the markers are indicated by the raised letter *m*.

> Áar wę̃yn^m mâ qabtay?
> Áar weyni^m mâ qabtay?

> Áar iyo gõol^m mâ qabteen?
> Áar iyo gooli^m mâ qabteen?

When a nominal cluster, taken as a unit, stands in neutral, closed or concatenated configuration there is no case differentiation in its marker, e.g.

> Wúxuu (wâxa uu) qabtay áar wę̃yn.
> 'He caught (ˈ)a big male lion(ˈ).'

> Wâxa qabtáy áar wę̃yn.
> '(ˈ)A big male lion(ˈ) caught him (etc.).'

> Áar wę̃yn bàa wįil qabtay.
> 'A boy caught (ˈ)a big male lion(ˈ).'

> Áar wę̃yn bàa wįil qabtáy.
> '(ˈ)A big male lion(ˈ) caught a boy.'

> Áar wę̃yn iyo gõol bày qabteen.
> 'They caught (ˈ)a big male lion and a lioness(ˈ).'

> Áar wę̃yn iyo gõol bàa qabtáy.
> '(ˈ)A big male lion and a lioness(ˈ) caught him (etc.).'

It is clear from all the formulations relating to the neutral and closed configurations that the presence and the relative position of indicators play an important rôle in the case system in Somali.

The concept of configuration is extended here to all the items which occur as N units, if in the definitions given above we replace the word noun by any of these items. It must be observed in this connection that the subj.pron. and the impers.pron. are always in open configuration and are always in case B, while the obj.pron.I and II, which also occur only in open configuration, are always in case A.

Although not directly related to the presence of indicators and their relative position in the sentence, the concept of setting is relevant to the concept of configuration and for this reason is mentioned here. In AN 64a three settings are recognized in nouns:

(i)	simple setting	when the noun does not form part of a nom.cl.
(ii)	subordinate setting	
	(a) subordinate-genitival	when the noun is dependent on an item other than any of those given under (b) below
	(b) subordinate-postnumeral	when the noun is dependent on a card.num., appr.num., unsp.num. or the inter.w.VI.
(iii)	integrated setting	when the noun forms part of a nom.cl. but is not in a subordinate setting

In this article the concept of setting is extended to those other items which can occur as N units; the para-nom.cl. is treated as an equivalent of the nom.cl. for the purposes of the above definition.

The concepts of configuration and of setting are used in the annotations of examples in Sections VII and XII. In this connection note the following abbreviations:

neu.cfg.	= neutral configuration	smp.stg.	= simple setting
clo.cfg.	= closed "	sub.gnt.stg.	= subordinate genitival setting
cct.cfg.	= concatenated "	sub.pnl.stg.	= subordinate postnumeral setting
ope.cfg.	= open "	intg.stg.	= integrated setting

Note that the division into types A and B in the forms of the def.art.gen., def.art.rem., dem., poss.def. and attr. is related to their distribution in different settings, configurations and cases. For the characteristics of forms A and B in these word classes see AN 64a: 118-120 and 127.

Section VI

SEMANTIC FUNCTIONS OF STRUCTURES IN WHICH INDICATORS OCCUR

It is very difficult, if not impossible, to describe the semantic functions of indicators in isolation. These functions have to be treated in relation to the syntactic structures of which the indicators are integral components and which are set out in detail in Table III, Section VII.

The description of the semantic functions of these structures as such (i.e. in abstraction from the lexical meaning of the constituent N and V units) includes, of necessity, the semantic functions of indicators.

The syntactic structures in which indicators occur have a number of specific types of semantic function which are described in this section. It is convenient to deal separately with (a) those structures which contain a V unit and (b) those which do not.

The types of semantic function in structures (a) are given in the list below:

STATEMENT	as contrasted with question or command.
ELICITIVE QUESTION	i.e. one to which an answer containing specific information is expected.
POLAR QUESTION	i.e. one to which the answer "yes" or "no" is normally expected.
ENCOURAGEMENT TO ACT	i.e. encouraging the listener to perform the action denoted by the V unit.
ENCOURAGEMENT TO AGREE	i.e. suggestion that the listener ought to agree with what the speaker is saying.
SUGGESTION OF LIKELIHOOD	i.e. suggestion that what the speaker is saying is likely to happen.
WISH	i.e. expression of a wish that what is denoted by the V unit should occur.
COMMAND	i.e. direct command addressed to the listener.
POSITIVENESS	as opposed to negativeness; note that the concept of positiveness is applied here to structures as such and not to the individual components. Thus *Wuu imán wgaỹey* 'He failed to come' is regarded as positive in spite of the negative meaning of the verb. Similarly, *Wàan maqlay ínaanu imán* 'I heard that he did not come' is regarded as positive in spite of the fact that the para-nom.cl.I, *ínaanu imán* 'that he did not come' is negative.
NEGATIVENESS	i.e. negation; note that, as in the case of positiveness, the concept of negativeness is applied here to structures and not to their individual components.

EMPHASIS

i.e. emphasis on a particular component of the structure; note that in the formulations in Table III in Section VII such emphasized components are placed between two exclamation marks in accordance with the practice introduced in HE 65. Although the term emphasis may seem self-evident its use in this article requires some comment. I use it in the sense, suggested by Hetzron (HE 74b), of "focussing (*mise en relief, Hervorhebung*)" which elevates "the communicational importance of an element above the level of the rest of the sentence." This function is clear in such contrastive sentences as:

(!)Xâsan(!) bâa yǫqâan.
'(!)Xasan(!) knows him (etc.).'

Xasan wâa (!)yǫqaan(!).
'Xasan (!)knows(!) him (etc.).'

The degree of the emphasizing function may differ according to various characteristics of the individual components of the ISC, but it is extremely difficult to calibrate it. The most significant and successful attempt at unravelling such semantic nuances is found in HE 65. In some cases, especially in longer sentences where a temporal expression receives emphasis, its degree is so attenuated that doubts may arise as to its presence. An interesting comment on this problem is provided by Zholkovsky (ZH 71: 129-136), who describes the emphasizing function as "logical accent," the presence of which is an obligatory feature of most Somali sentences. He remarks that this logical accent can undergo semantic erosion (*razmïvaetsya*), a linguistic phenomenon to which parallels can be found in other languages.

HERALDING

which consists of announcing at the beginning of the structure that the emphasized component will occur at the end of it. Note that this kind of "announcing" is dealt with in HE 74b. Hetzron describes the Somali structures which have this function within the framework of his Presentative Movement, a phenomenon which, as he demonstrates, has parallels in numerous languages, and the motivation for which, it seems, may amount to a language universal.

The types of semantic functions present in structures (b) are given below:

STATEMENT   as in structures (a).
ELICITIVE QUESTION   "   "   "   "
POLAR QUESTION   "   "   "   "
EMPHASIS   "   "   "   "
HERALDING   "   "   "   "

IDENTIFICATION

can only be defined in relation to certain other semantic functions. (a) If the sentence is a statement, this function consists of an assertion that someone or something is what is denoted by the emphasised N unit, e.g. *Nînkanu waa yǫâas.* 'This man is (!)a chieftain(!).' Note that the subject in such sentences is often omitted, e.g. *Waa yǫâas.* '[He] is (!)a chieftain(!).' (b) If the sentence is an elicitive question, this function consists of an inquiry in answer to which a statement concerning the identity or some identifying characteristics of someone or something is expected, e.g. *Wâa yǫaaskêe?* '(!)Which chieftain(!) is he?' (c) If the sentence is a polar question, this function consists of an inquiry whether someone or something is or is not what is denoted by the emphasized N unit e.g. *Nînkanu ma yǫâas bâa?* 'Is this man (!)a chieftain(!)?', *Ma yǫâas bâa?* 'Is [he] (!)a chieftain(!)?' For further information see AN 64a: 137-140.

SPECIFICATION OF NECESSITY again, can only be defined in relation to certain other semantic functions. (a) If the sentence is a statement, this function consists of an assertion that what is specified by the emphasized N unit is necessary or obligatory, e.g. *Waa* (!)*ìnuu yìmaaddaa*(!) 'It is necessary (or obligatory) (!)that he should come(!).' (b) If the sentence is a polar question, this function consists of an inquiry whether what is specified by the emphasized N unit is necessary or obligatory, e.g. *Ma ìnuu yìmaaddaa bàa?* 'Is it necessary (or obligatory) (!)that he should come(!)?'

It is important to observe that the structures in which indicators occur always have two or more semantic functions which are mutually compatible. Some of these structures, however, also have semantic functions which are mutually exclusive, and the choice between them is determined by certain specific characteristics of the emphasized unit in the structure.

Such mutually exclusive functions are:

(i) ELICITIVE QUESTION and STATEMENT.

(ii) SPECIFICATION OF NECESSITY and IDENTIFICATION.

In (i) the choice is determined as follows: When the emphasized unit consists of an inter.def., any inter.w. or a nom.aggr.II, the structure has the function of an elicitive question, e.g. *Kèe bày dòonaysaa?* '(!)Which one(!) does she want?.' When the emphasized unit does not consist of any of these items, the structure in which such a choice is possible has the function of a statement, e.g. *Dhàr bày dòonaysaa.* 'She wants (!)clothes(!).'

Similarly, in (ii) the choice is determined as follows: When the emphasized unit consists of a para-nom.cl.I, the structure in which such a choice is possible has the function of specification of necessity, e.g. *Waa ìnuu yìmaaddaa.* 'It is necessary (or obligatory) (!)that he should come(!).' When the emphasized unit does not consist of a para-nom.cl.I, the structure in which such a choice is possible has the function of identification, e.g. *Waa ugàas.* '[He] is (!)a chieftain(!).'

Section VII

STRUCTURES IN WHICH INDICATORS OCCUR: INDICATOR CENTRED CORES

It was said in Section I that every fully formed sentence, with the exception of the types listed in Section X, must have at least one indicator. This statement, however, requires some amplification. The presence of particular indicators in the sentence is always concomitant with the presence of certain other items which can be said to form the essential minimum environment of these indicators. Such items have a fixed order in relation to each other and to the indicators. When describing the essential minimum environment of indicators it is necessary to include in these structures the indicators themselves and this is done in Table III below. The term indicator centred core (abbreviated to ICC) will be used here to subsume both indicators and their essential minimum environment. It follows from the above formulations that indicators cannot occur outside their ICCs.

ICCs as structures have semantic functions which are described in Section VI. The distribution of these functions is given in Table III.

In interpreting the formulaic statements provided in that table the following points should be borne in mind:

(a) There are only four types of components in the ICCs: N units, V units, the neg.ptc. *aan-*[!] and indicators.

(b) The indicators and the neg.ptc. *aan-*[!] are written in full. The optional variants of indicators are omitted but the formulaic statements refer to these variants as well. It should be noted, however, that the optional variants of *bàa* do not normally occur when the emphasized N unit is preceded by ind. *ma*! or when it consists of an inter.def., any inter.w., nom.aggr.II or a subs.pron.

(c) The raised letter c (as in N1^C, V1^C etc.) indicates that the two items marked with it are in concord with each other. For references to concord rules see Section II, the entry on noun; see also BE 53, AN 61, AN 68 and AN 69.

(d) Even those verbal forms which belong to invariable paradigms, i.e. those which are the same in all persons (e.g. neg.pres.-past gen.), are regarded as capable of concord with N units. The formal test of concord in such cases is the potentiality of concord in the corresponding forms of variable paradigms, i.e. those which have different forms in different persons of the paradigm (e.g. pres.gen.ext.).

(e) When the N unit is a para-nom.cl.I vacillation occurs in the gender of the V unit in concord with it. Especially when the V unit consists of a form of the verb *dhàc* (Z) 'to happen', *jìr* (Z) 'to be' or *muuqò* (AN) 'to appear, to seem', there is a marked tendency for the para-nom.cl.I to be treated, from the point of view of concord, as if it were a sg.f. rather than sg.m. noun, e.g. *Wàxa muuqatà ìnay yìmaaddèen.* 'It appears that they have come' (Lit. 'That they have come appears.'). Such a preference may be due to the fact that in Somali 3sg.f. form of the subj. pron. is frequently used in impersonal constructions, e.g. *Shàlay bày ahayd.* 'It was yesterday.'

(f) When the ind. *wàxa* and a V unit precede an N unit, the concord between the V and N units is open to the following type of vacillation: 3sg.m. forms of the verb can occur as optional alternatives to 3sg.f. forms, except when the noun in concord denotes one person of female sex or one animal distinctly perceived as being of female sex, e.g. *hàl* 'she-camel'. Vacillation is particularly common when the noun is fem.coll. e.g. *Wàxa timì èrgo* 'A delegation came' or *Wàxa yimì èrgo* (The same meaning.).

(g) When the ind. *bàa* (*ayàa, yàa*), *miyàa, waa*!- or *wàxa* (*waxàa*) are followed by the neg.ptc. *aan* they combine with it into the following contracted forms: *bàan* (*ayàan, yàan*), *miyàan, waan*!-, *wàxàan* (*waxàan*). For an account of "contraction" in Somali see AN 64a: 114-117 and MU 56: 20-23.

(h) When the indicators given in (g) above are followed by the neg.ptc. *aan*! and a subj.pron. they combine with these items into the following contracted forms:[11]

    bàanan

    bàanad

    bàanu

    bàanay

    bàannan (*bàannaan*)

    bàynan (*bàynaan*)

    bàydan (*bàydaan*) (*bàynad*)

    bàanay

   (*ayàanan*)

   (*ayàanad*)

     etc.

   (*yàanan*)

   (*yàanad*)

     etc.

---

[11]Note that there are dialectal variations, even within the Standard dialect type, in the forms of these combinations; see, for example, MO 55: 285.

míyáanan

míyáanad

etc.

wáanan

wáanad

etc.

wáxaanan

wáxaanad

etc.

(i) When the indicators listed in (g) above are followed by a subj.pron. they combine
with it into the following contracted forms:

báan

báad

búu

báy

báannu (báan)

báynu

báad (báydín, báa)

báy

ayáan

ayáad

etc.

yáan

yáad

etc.

míyáan

míyáad

etc.

*waan*ⁱ

*waad*ⁱ

etc.

wáxaan (waxáan)

wáxaad (waxáad)

wúxuu (wuxúu)

wáxay (waxáy)

etc.

Note that the uncontracted sequences of *wáxa* and a subj.pron. can also occur:

wáxa aan

wáxa aad

wáxa uu

wáxa ay

etc.

(j) When the ind. *yaan⌐* is followed by a subj.pron. they combine into the following contracted forms:

yáanan (*yaan⌐*)

yáanad (*yaad⌐*)

yáanu (*yuu⌐*)

yáanay (*yay⌐*, *yey⌐*)

yáannan (*yáannaan*, *yaannu⌐*)

yáynan (*yáynaan*, *yéynan*, *yéynaan*, *yaynu⌐*, *yeynu⌐*)

yáydan (*yáydaan*, *yéydan*, *yéydaan*, *yáynad*, *yéynad*, *yaad⌐*)

yáanay (*yay⌐*, *yey⌐*)

(k) Some ICCs occur rarely or very rarely; they are marked with *ɼ* or *ɼ̱* respectively.[12]

(1) The presence of particular semantic functions is shown by the sign + placed in the column headed by the appropriate designations which are explained in Section VI. Thus for example the structure *wáxa aan⌐* N2^C V2^C !N4! has the following semantic functions:

I. It emphasizes what is denoted by N4.

II. It shows that the sentence is a statement.

III. It shows that the emphasized item comes at the end of the structure.

IV. It shows that the sentence is negative.

Similarly, *waa⌐* !N8! has the following semantic functions:

I. It emphasizes what is denoted by N8.

II. It shows that the sentence is a statement if N8 is not an inter.def., an inter.w. or a nom.aggr.II.

III. It shows that the sentence is an elicitive question if N8 is one of the items enumerated in II above.

IV. It shows that the sentence contains a specific assertion concerning the identity of what is denoted by N8 if N8 is not a para-nom.cl.I.

V. It shows that the sentence contains a specific assertion that what is denoted by N8 is obligatory or necessary if N8 is a para-nom.cl.I.

---

[12]The relative frequency of the commonly occurring ICCs varies according to the context. The ICCs which are elicitive or polar questions, for example, are found more often in a dialogue than in a narrative. It is highly relevant, from the point of view of the study of Presentative Movement (HE 74b), that the ICCs which contain the ind. *wáxa* are much favoured in radio news bulletins. I have found that in some of them every sentence contained the ind. *wáxa*. Since the introduction of the national orthography in 1972 this practice has also been adopted by journalists.

TABLE III

THE STRUCTURES AND SEMANTIC FUNCTIONS OF ICCs
Part One

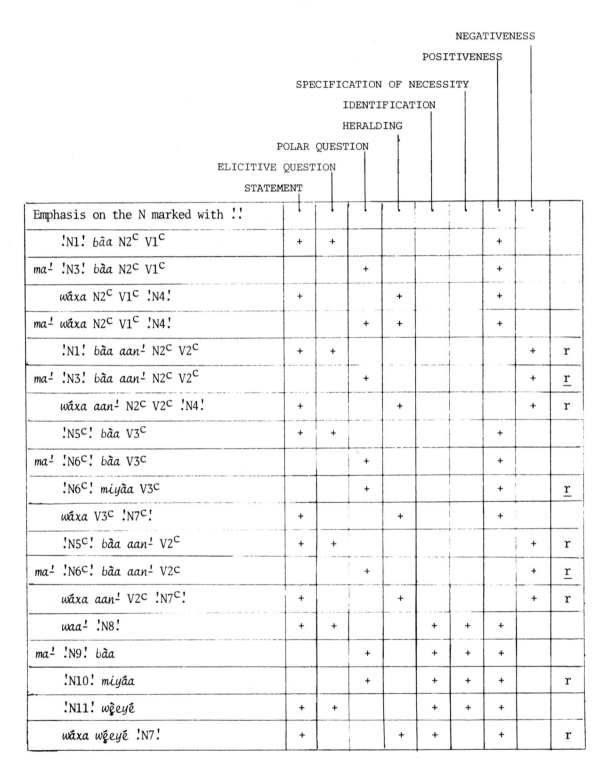

Emphasis on the N marked with !ˎ!	STATEMENT	ELICITIVE QUESTION	POLAR QUESTION	HERALDING	IDENTIFICATION	SPECIFICATION OF NECESSITY	POSITIVENESS	NEGATIVENESS	
!N1! *bāa* $N2^C$ $V1^C$	+	+					+		
ma-! !N3! *bāa* $N2^C$ $V1^C$			+				+		
wáxa $N2^C$ $V1^C$!N4!	+			+			+		
ma-! *wáxa* $N2^C$ $V1^C$!N4!			+	+			+		
!N1! *bāa aan*-! $N2^C$ $V2^C$	+	+						+	r
ma-! !N3! *bāa aan*-! $N2^C$ $V2^C$			+					+	r̲
wáxa aan-! $N2^C$ $V2^C$!N4!	+			+				+	r
!$N5^C$! *bāa* $V3^C$	+	+					+		
ma-! !$N6^C$! *bāa* $V3^C$			+				+		
!$N6^C$! *miyàa* $V3^C$			+				+		r̲
wáxa $V3^C$!$N7^C$!	+			+			+		
!$N5^C$! *bāa aan*-! $V2^C$	+	+						+	r
ma-! !$N6^C$! *bāa aan*-! $V2^C$			+					+	r̲
wáxa aan-! $V2^C$!$N7^C$!	+			+				+	r
waa-! !N8!	+	+			+	+	+		
ma-! !N9! *bāa*			+		+	+	+		
!N10! *miyáa*			+		+	+	+		r
!N11! *wẹeyê*	+	+			+	+	+		
wáxa wẹeyê !N7!	+			+	+		+		r

TABLE III

Part Two

Emphasis on the V marked with !!	STATEMENT	POLAR QUESTION	ENCOURAGEMENT TO ACT	ENCOURAGEMENT TO AGREE	SUGGESTION OF LIKELIHOOD	WISH	COMMAND	POSITIVENESS	NEGATIVENESS	
$ma^{\underline{!}}$!V1!		+						+		
$ma^{\underline{!}}$!V4!		+	+					+		r
$ma^{\underline{!}}$!V5!	+								+	
$soo^{\underline{!}}$ $ma^{\underline{!}}$!V5!		+		+					+	
$miyàa$ N2^C !V1^C!		+						+		
$miyàa$ $aan^{\underline{!}}$ N2^C !V2^C!		+							+	
$soo^{\underline{!}}$ $miyàa$ $aan^{\underline{!}}$ N2^C !V2^C!		+		+					+	r
$soo^{\underline{!}}$!V6!	+				+			+		r
$waa^{\underline{!}}$!V1!	+							+		
$waa^{\underline{!}}$ $aan^{\underline{!}}$ N2^C !V2^C!	+								+	r
$yaan^{\underline{!}}$ N2^C !V7^C!						+			+	
$ha^{\underline{!}}$!V8!						+		+		
$ha^{\underline{!}}$!V9!							+		+	

The formulaic statements given in Table III above are illustrated in the remaining part of this section by very short sentences with a limited vocabulary. The aim of these examples is merely to demonstrate how these statements were arrived at and how they can be applied. More varied examples, drawn from wider contexts, are given in Section XII.

The recurrent vocabulary items in the examples below are as follows:

$àwr$ (n.m.)	'a he-camel'
$kèen$ (v.Z)	'to bring'
$maxáy$ (inter.w.II)	'what?'
uu (3sg.m.subj.pron.)	'he'

Each example is given a serial number and is annotated. Note that in the translation of examples the semantic function of heralding later emphasis is not shown owing to the difficulties of rendering it in English without recourse to circumlocution; its presence or its absence can be deduced from the formulae at the end of each annotation.

/1/   Áwr búu keenay.
       'He brought (!)a he-camel(!).'

       àwr (smp.stg., clo.cfg.)
       búu = bàa + uu
       bàa (ind.)
       uu (3sg.m.subj.pron.)
       keenay (3sg.m.past gen.ext.)

       ICC = !N1! bàa N2^C V1^C
             N1 = àwr
             N2 = uu
             V1 = keenay

/2/   Muxùu keenay?
       '(!)What(!) did he bring?'

       muxùu = maxáy + bàa + uu^{13}
       maxáy (smp.stg., clo.cfg.)
       bàa
       uu   as in /1/
       keenay

       ICC = !N1! bàa N2^C V1^C
             N1 = maxáy
             N2 =   as in /1/
             V1 =

/3/   Ma àwr búu keenay?
       'Did he bring (!)a he-camel(!)?'

       ma! (ind.); ma (pos.var.)
       àwr
       búu
       bàa   as in /1/
       uu
       keenay

       ICC = ma! !N3! bàa N2^C V1^C
             N3 = àwr
             N2 =   as in /1/
             V1 =

/4/   Wúxuu keenay àwr.
       'He brought (!)a he-camel(!).'

       wúxuu = wáxa uu
       wáxa (ind.)
       uu (3sg.m.subj.pron.)
       keenay (3sg.m.past gen.ext.)
       àwr (smp.stg., neu.cfg.)

       ICC = wáxa N2^C V1^C !N4!
             N2 = uu
             V1 = keenay
             N4 = àwr

---

[13]Note that uncontracted sequences of maxáy + bàa do not occur.

/5/   Ma wúxuu keenay àwr?
       'Did he bring (!)a he-camel(!)?'

       ma⸍ (ind.); ma (pos.var.)
       wúxuu
       wáxa
       uu   as in /4/
       keenay
       àwr

       ICC = ma⸍ wáxa N2^C V1^C !N4!
            N2 =
            V1 = as in /4/
            N4 =

/6/   Àwr báanu keenín.
       'He did not bring (!)a he-camel(!).'

       àwr (smp.stg., clo.cfg.)
       báanu = bàa + aan⸍ + uu
       bàa (ind.)
       aan⸍ (neg.ptc.)
       uu (3sg.m.subj.pron.)
       keenín (neg.pres.-past gen.)

       ICC = !N1! bàa aan⸍ N2^C V2^C
            N1 = àwr
            N2 = uu
            V2 = keenín

/7/   Ma àwr báanu keenín?
       'Did he not bring (!)a he-camel(!)?'

       ma⸍ (ind.); ma (pos.var.)
       àwr
       báanu
       bàa
       aan⸍   as in /6/
       uu
       keenín

       ICC = ma⸍ !N3! bàa aan⸍ N2^C V2^C
            N3 = àwr
            N2 =
            V2 = as in /6/

/8/   Wáxaanu keenín àwr.
       'He did not bring (!)a he-camel(!).'

       wáxaanu = wáxa + aan⸍ + uu
       wáxa (ind.)
       aan⸍ (neg.ptc.)
       uu (3sg.m.subj.pron.)
       keenín (neg.pres.-past gen.)
       àwr (smp.stg., neu.cfg.)

       ICC = wáxa aan⸍ N2^C V2^C !N4!
            N2 = uu
            V2 = keenín
            N4 = àwr

/9/   Àwr bàa keenáy.
       '(!)A he-camel(!) brought it (etc.).'

ãwɾ (smp.stg., clo.cfg.)
bãa (ind.)
keenãy (3sg.m.past gen.res.)

ICC = !N5^C! bãa V3^C
    N5 = ãwɾ
    V3 = keenãy

/10/   Ma ãwɾ bãa keenãy?
     'Did (!)a he-camel(!) bring it (etc.)?'

ma$^!$ (ind.); ma (pos.var.)
ãwɾ
bãa   as in /9/
keenãy

ICC = ma$^!$!N6^C! bãa V3^C
    N6 = ãwɾ
    V3 = keenãy

/11/   Àwɾ míyãa keenãy?
     'Did (!)a he-camel(!) bring it (etc.)?'

ãwɾ (smp.stg.clo.cfg.)
míyãa (ind.)
keenãy (3sg.m.past gen.res.)

ICC = !N6^C! míyãa V3^C
    N6 =
    V3 =   as in /10/

/12/   Wãxa keenãy ãwɾ.
     '(!)A he-camel(!) brought it (etc.).'

wãxa (ind.)
keenãy (3sg.m.past gen.res.)
ãwɾ (smp.stg., neu.cfg.)

ICC = wãxa V3^C !N7^C!
    V3 = keenãy
    N7 = ãwɾ

/13/   Àwɾ bãan kᶒenín.
     '(!)A he-camel(!) did not bring it (etc.).'

ãwɾ (smp.stg., clo.cfg.)
bãan = bãa + aan$^!$
bãa (ind.)
aan$^!$ (neg.ptc.)
kᶒenín (neg.pres.-past gen.)

ICC = !N5^C! bãa aan$^!$ V2^C
    N5 = ãwɾ
    V2 = kᶒenín

/14/   Ma ãwɾ bãan kᶒenín?
     'Did not (!)a he-camel(!) bring it (etc.)?'

ma$^!$ (ind.); ma (pos.var.)
ãwɾ
bãan   as in /13/
bãa
aan$^!$
kᶒenín

ICC = $ma^{\underline{!}}$ $!N6^{C}!$ $b\tilde{a}a$ $aan^{\underline{!}}$ $V2^{C}$
　　　N6 = $\tilde{a}wr$
　　　V2 = $k\underset{\smile}{e}en\tilde{\imath}n$

/15/　*Wắxắan* $k\underset{\smile}{e}en\tilde{\imath}n$ $\tilde{a}wr.$
　　　'(!)A he-camel(!) did not bring it (etc.).'

wắxắan = *wắxa* + $aan^{\underline{!}}$
wắxa (ind.)
$aan^{\underline{!}}$ (neg.ptc.)
$k\underset{\smile}{e}en\tilde{\imath}n$ (neg.pres.-past gen.)
$\tilde{a}wr$ (smp.stg., neu.cfg.)

ICC = *wắxa* $aan^{\underline{!}}$ $V2^{C}$ $!N7^{C}!$
　　　V2 = $k\underset{\smile}{e}en\tilde{\imath}n$
　　　N7 = $\tilde{a}wr$

/16/　*Waa* $\tilde{a}wr.$
　　　'It is (!)a he-camel(!).'

$waa^{\underline{!}}$ (ind.); *waa* (pos.var.)
$\tilde{a}wr$ (smp.stg., neu.cfg.)

ICC = $waa^{\underline{!}}$ $!N8!$
　　　N8 = $\tilde{a}wr$

/17/　*Ma* $\tilde{a}wr$ $b\tilde{a}a?$
　　　'Is it (!)a he-camel(!)?'

$ma^{\underline{!}}$ (ind.); *ma* (pos.var.)
$\tilde{a}wr$ (smp.stg., clo.cfg.)
$b\tilde{a}a$ (ind.)

ICC = $ma^{\underline{!}}$ $!N9!$ $b\tilde{a}a$
　　　N9 = $\tilde{a}wr$

/18/　*Ằwr* *míyằa?*
　　　'Is it (!)a he-camel(!)?'

$\tilde{a}wr$ (smp.stg., clo.cfg.)
míyằa (ind.)

ICC = $!N10!$ *míyằa*
　　　N10 = $\tilde{a}wr$

/19/　*Waa* $\tilde{\imath}nuu$ *keenaa.*
　　　'It is necessary (!)that he should bring it (etc.)(!).'

$waa^{\underline{!}}$ (ind.); *waa* (pos.var.)
$\tilde{\imath}nuu$ *keenaa* (para-nom.cl.I/smp.stg., neu.cfg.)
$\tilde{\imath}nuu$ = $\tilde{\imath}n$ + *uu*
$\tilde{\imath}n$ (decl.ptc.) 'that'
uu (3sg.m.subj.pron.)
keenaa (3sg.m.pres.gen.dvg.B)

ICC = $waa^{\underline{!}}$ $!N8!$
　　　N8 = $\tilde{\imath}nuu$ *keenaa*

/20/　*Ma* $\tilde{\imath}nuu$ *keenaa* $b\tilde{a}a?$
　　　'Is it necessary (!)that he should bring it (etc.)(!)?'

$ma^{\underline{!}}$ (ind.); *ma* (pos.var.)
$\tilde{\imath}nuu$ *keenaa* (para-nom.cl.I/smp.stg., clo.cfg.)

ínuu
ín
uu   as in /19/
keenaa
bãa (ind.)

ICC = ma⁻ ͥ !N9! bãa
    N9 = ínuu keenaa

/21/ Àwr wẹ̃eyê.
      'It is (!)a he-camel(!).'

àwr (smp.stg., neu.cfg.)
wẹ̃eyê (ind.)

ICC = !N11! wẹ̃eyê
    N11 = àwr

/22/ Ínuu keenaa wẹ̃eyê.
      'It is necessary (!)that he should bring it (etc.)(!).'

ínuu keenaa (para-nom.cl.I/smp.stg., neu.cfg.)
ínuu
ín   as in /19/
uu
keenaa
wẹ̃eyê (ind.)

ICC = !N11! wẹ̃eyê
    N11 = ínuu keenaa

/23/ Wãxa wẹ̃eyê àwr.
      'It is (!)a he-camel(!).'

wãxa (ind.)
wẹ̃eyê (ind.)
àwr (smp.stg., neu.cfg.)

ICC = wãxa wẹ̃eyê !N7!
    N7 = àwr

/24/ Mã keenay?
      '(!)Did(!) he (etc.) (!)bring(!) it (etc.)?'

ma⁻ ͥ (ind.); mã (pos.var.)
keenay (3sg.m.past gen.ext.)

ICC = ma⁻ ͥ !V1!
    V1 = keenay

/25/ Ma kẹ̃entid?
      It is very diffidult to translate this sentence into English without recourse to
      circumlocution. The nearest equivalent might be: 'Why don't you bring it (etc.)?' or
      'It might be a good thing for you to bring it (etc.)!' Note that in Somali this is
      a positive rhetorical question encouraging the listener to perform the action denoted
      by the emphasized V unit.

ma⁻ ͥ (ind.); ma (pos.var.)
kẹ̃entid (2sg.rhet.)

ICC = ma⁻ ͥ !N4!
    V4 = kẹ̃entid

Note that in the majority of examples of this ICC which I have found, the ind. ma⁻ ͥ is
followed by and combined with a subj.pron. Thus the more normal version of this

sentence would be *Maad ǩeentid?*, where *maad* = *ma⸴* (ind.) + *aad* (2sg.subj.pron.). Both
have the same meaning.

/26/ *Mǎ ǩeenín.*
'He (etc.) (!)did not bring(!) it (etc.).'

ma⸴ (ind.); *mǎ* (pos.var.)
ǩeenín (neg.pres.-past gen.)

ICC = *ma⸴* !V5!
   V5 = *ǩeenín*

/27/ *Soo mǎ ǩeenín?*
'(!)Did(!) he (etc.) (!)not bring(!) it (etc.)?' This sentence also implies:
'Of course, he (etc.) brought it (etc.).'

soo⸴ (ind.); *soo* (pos.var.)
ma⸴ (ind.); *mǎ* (pos.var.)
ǩeenín (neg.pres.-past gen.)

ICC = *soo⸴ ma⸴* !V5!
   V5 = *ǩeenín*

/28/ *Miyǔu keenay?*
'(!)Did(!) he (!)bring(!) it (etc.)?'

miyǔu = *miyǎa* + *uu*
miyǎa (ind.)
uu (3sg.m.subj.pron.)
keenay (3sg.m.past gen.ext.)

ICC = *miyǎa* N2^{C} !V1^{C}!
    N2 = *uu*
    V1 = *keenay*

/29/ *Miyǎanu ǩeenín?*
'(!)Did(!) he (!)not bring(!) it (etc.)?'

miyǎanu = *miyǎa* + *aan⸴* + *uu*
miyǎa (ind.)
aan⸴ (neg.ptc.)
uu (3sg.m.subj.pron.)
ǩeenín (neg.pres.-past gen.)

ICC = *miyǎa aan⸴* N2^{C} !V2^{C}!
    N2 = *uu*
    N2 = *ǩeenín*

/30/ *Soo miyǎanu ǩeenín?*
'(!)Did(!) he (!)not bring(!) it (etc.)?' This sentence also implies:
'Of course, he brought it (etc.).'

soo⸴ (ind.); *soo* (pos.var.)
miyǎanu
miyǎa
aan⸴   as in /29/
uu
ǩeenín

ICC = *soo⸴ miyǎa aan⸴* N2^{C} !V2^{C}!
  N2 =
  V2 = as in /29/

Note that this ICC is very rare and some speakers regard it as grammatically substandard.

/31/ *Sŏo keenee.*
      'He (etc.) (⸗)is likely to bring(⸗) it (etc.).'

   soo⸗ (ind.); *sŏo* (pos.var.)
   keenee (3sg.m. or 1sg.poten.)

   ICC = *soo⸗* ⸗V6⸗
      V6 = *keenee*

/32/ *Wăa keenay.*
      'He (etc.) (⸗)brought(⸗) it (etc.).'

   waa⸗ (ind.); *wăa* (pos.var.)
   keenay (3sg.m. or 1sg.past gen.ext.)

   ICC = *waa⸗* ⸗V1⸗
      V1 = *keenay*

/33/ *Wăanu keenín.*
      'He (⸗)did not bring(⸗) it (etc.).'

   wăanu = *waa⸗* + *aan⸗* + *uu*
   waa⸗ (ind.)
   aan⸗ (neg.ptc.)
   uu (3sg.m.subj.pron.)
   keenín (neg.pres.-past gen.)

   ICC = *waa⸗ aan⸗* N2^C V2^C
      N2 = *uu*
      V2 = *keenín*

/34/ *Yăanu keenin⸗*
      '(⸗)Let(⸗) him (⸗)not bring(⸗) it (etc.)⸗' *or* '(⸗)May(⸗) he (⸗)not bring(⸗) it (etc.)⸗'

   yăanu = *yaan⸗* + *uu*
   yaan⸗ (ind.)
   uu (3sg.m.subj.pron.)
   keenin (neg.opt.)

   ICC = *yaan⸗* N2^C ⸗V7^C⸗
      N2 = *uu*
      V7 = *keenin*

/35/ *Hă keeno⸗*
      '(⸗)Let(⸗) him (etc.) (⸗)bring(⸗) it (etc.)⸗' *or* '(⸗)May(⸗) he (⸗)bring(⸗) it (etc.)⸗'

   ha⸗ (ind.); *hă* (pos.var.)
   keeno (3sg.m.optat.)

   ICC = *ha⸗* ⸗V8⸗
      V8 = *keeno*

/36/ *Ha keenína⸗*
      '(⸗)Do not bring(⸗) it (etc.)⸗'

   ha⸗ (ind.); *ha* (pos.var.)
   keenína (2pl.neg.imper.)

   ICC = *ha⸗* ⸗V9⸗

As far as I have been able to ascertain, Table III in this section gives all the ICCs in the language. Note, however, that I have left out the structure exemplified in MJ 56: 36 by *hăsha ma bădh misé bădh* '[as for] the she-camel is it [the first] half [that I should speak about first] or [the other] half?'. My reason for doing so is that this structure may be regarded as elliptical, as suggested in MU 56: 81. If this view is taken, the *ma bâdh* part could be assumed to represent the two initial components of one of the following ICCs: *ma!* *!N3! bâa* N2^C V1^C, *ma! !N6^C! bâa* V3^C or *ma! !N9! bâa*.

It should also be observed that in the commonly occurring expression *wâa i kân* 'here I am' (used in answer to a call) the ICC is assumed to be *waa !N8!*, where N8 = *kân* (dem.m.). The component *i* (1sg.obj.pron.I) 'me' is regarded as extraneous to the ICC. I am aware that this is a tentative solution.

Section VIII
EXTENSIONS OF INDICATOR CENTRED CORES

In some sentences there are groups of words which precede ICCs and might be considered as their extensions. These extensions are identical with the initial parts of certain ICCs and are as follows:

  (i)   !N1! *bâa*

  (ii) !N1! *bâa* N2^C

The N units in these extensions normally refer to time. The ICCs which can be preceded by such extensions are:

  (a) those which begin with !N1!

  (b)   "   "   "   " *wâxa* and contain V1^C

  (c)   "   "   "   " !N5^C! "   "   V3^C

  (d)   "   "   "   " *wâxa* "   "   V3^C

The following combinations are possible:

  (i) + ⎧ (a)
         ⎪ (b)   (ii) + ⎧ (a)
         ⎨ (c)   ⎨ (b)
         ⎪ (d)   ⎩
         ⎩

Examples:

(i) + (a)   *Mârkaasâa l̰ibâax bûu arkay.*
            '(!)Then(!) he saw (!)a lion(!).'

            mârkaasâa = mârkâas + bâa
            mârkâas (nom.aggr.I/smp.stg.,clo.cfg.) 'then' = *mâr* + *kâas*
            mâr (n.m.) 'time', 'point in time'
            kâas (dem.m.) 'that'
            bâa (ind.)
            l̰ibâax (n.m.) 'a lion', - - - (smp.stg., clo.cfg.)
            bûu = bâa + uu
            bâa (ind.)
            uu (3sg.m.subj.pron.)
            ârag (v.Z) 'to see'; *arkay* (3sg.m.past gen.ext.)

(i) + (b)   *Mârkaasâa wûxuu arkay l̰ibâax.*
            '(!)Then(!) he saw (!)a lion(!).'

            mârkaasâa, as in (i) + (a)
            wûxuu = wâxa + uu
            wâxa (ind.)

uu (3sg.m.subj.pron.)
áɾag, aɾkay, as in (i) + (a)
ɭ̣baax (n.m.) 'a lion'; - - - (smp.stg., neu.cfg.)

(i) + (c)   *Máɾkaasàa ɭ̣baax bàa aɾkáy.*
             '(!)Then(!) (!)a lion(!) saw him (etc.).'

             máɾkaasàa, as in (i) + (a)
             ɭ̣baax, as in (i) + (a)
             bàa (ind.
             áɾag (v.Z) 'to see'; *aɾkáy* (esg.m.past gen.res.)

(i) + (d)   *Máɾkaasàa wáxa aɾkáy ɭ̣baax.*
             '(!)Then(!) (!)a lion(!) saw him (etc.).'

             máɾkaasàa, as in (i) + (a)
             wáxa (ind.)
             áɾag; aɾkáy, as in (i) + (c)
             ɭ̣baax, as in (i) + (b)

(ii) + (a)   *Máɾkaasùu ɭ̣baax bùu aɾkay.*
             '(!)Then(!) he saw (!)a lion(!).'

             máɾkáas, as in (i) + (a)
             bùu = bàa + uu
             bàa (ind.)
             uu (3sg.m.subj.pron.)
             ɭ̣baax
             bùu   as in (i) + (a)
             áɾag, aɾkay

(ii) + (b)   *Máɾkaasùu wúxuu aɾkay ɭ̣baax.*
             '(!)Then(!) he saw (!)a lion(!).'

             máɾkaasùu, as in (ii) + (a)
             wúxuu, as in (i) + (b)
             áɾag, aɾkay, as in (i) + (a)
             ɭ̣baax, as in (i) + (b)

It should be noted that examples (i) + (a), (i) + (b), (ii) + (a) and (ii) + (b) are nearly synonymous with each other. The same applies to examples (i) + (c) and (i) + (d).

In the examples in which the ind. *wáxa* occurs, however, the ICCs have the function of heralding (see Section VI); in the other examples this function is absent.

Note that extensions of ICCs occur rarely and are almost totally restricted to a leisurely narrative style.

For further discussion of sentences with two indicators see HE 65: 124-126.[14]

---

[14]It might be appropriate to mention here that I am in complete agreement with the emendation of Line 76 of Text 22 in MU 56: 49 suggested in HE 65: 125. The text is faulty due to an error in transcription.

Section IX

INDICATOR CENTRED CORES AND SENTENCE NUCLEI

During the initial period of my investigation into the rôles of indicators in Somali, which began some years ago, I expected that ICCs could be established as sentence nuclei in the sense used by Guthrie, i.e. as the smallest irreducible parts of the sentence (GU 61: 2-3). This, however, did not prove feasible on account of the difficulties which arise from certain properties found in some sentence components which enter into ICCs. Let us consider some of the most important cases.

Although prep.ptcs. cannot be established as constant components of ICCs, in some sentences their deletion would render the utterance meaningless. Take, for example,

> *Cĕelkíi bûu kắ keenay.*

> 'He brought it (etc.) from (ː)the well(ː).'

If *kắ* 'from' is deleted in this sentence it no longer remains meaningful.

A similar difficulty arises in the case of what I shall describe as the lexically interdependent phrase (abbreviated to lex.int.phr.). A phrase of this kind is characterized by the fact that its components have a joint meaning which cannot be fully related to the meanings they usually have in other contexts. Some components of lex.int.phrs. can be separated from each other by another word or words and this is indicated by the sign .ː. in the examples below, while some must follow one another without the possibility of such separation and this is indicated by the sign ːː. In the examples below the "joint" meanings of lex.int.phrs. are compared with the usual meanings of their components.

> *ắqal* (n.m.)ːː *gắl* (v.Z) 'to begin cohabitation with one's bride or bridegroom'; cf.
> *ắqal* (n.m.) 'a house', 'a hut' and *gắl* (v.Z) 'to enter'

> *ʃarŏ* (n.m.pl.)ːː *gḛli* (v.IN) 'to interfere with'; cf. *ʃarŏ* (n.m.pl.) 'fingers' and
> *gḛli* (v.IN) 'to cause to enter'

> *kaː* (prep.ptc.).ː. *qáyb* (n.f.)ːː *gắl* (v.Z) 'to participate in [an activity]'; cf. *kaː*
> (prep.ptc.) 'in', 'from', *qáyb* (n.f.) 'a share [of something]' and *gắl* (v.Z) 'to
> enter'

> *kuː* (prep.ptc.).ː. *dhuʃŏ* (v.AN) 'to hit [someone or something] with [something]'; cf.
> *kuː* (prep.ptc.) 'with', 'by means of' and *dhuʃŏ* (v.AN) 'to pull'

There is also a similar problem when a verb which constitutes a V unit of an ICC is preceded by a noun used in what I shall refer to as preverbal mode (abbreviated to prev.mode). The formal characteristic of this mode is that the noun is immediately followed by a verb from which it cannot be separated by any other word; if we employ Zholkovsky's table of precedence of preverbal items the noun in prev.mode occupies position 11 (ZH 71: 222).

When a noun in prev.mode refers to a relative position in space it usually has a semantic function similar to that of such English words as 'near', 'among', 'under' etc. Consider, for example, the functions of the nouns *ắg* (n.f.) 'vicinity', *dhḛx* (n.f.) '[the] middle [part of something]' and *hôos* (n.f.) '[the] bottom [part of something]' in the sentences given below:

> *Aqalkíi bûu ắg ʃadhiistay.*

> 'He sat near (ː)the house(ː).'

> *Dắdkíi bûu dhḛx galay.*

> 'He went among (ː)the people(ː).' ('went', lit. 'entered')

> *Gḛedkíi bûu hôos jɡogsaday.*

> 'He stopped under (ː)the tree(ː).'

A noun which does not refer to a relative position in space, when it occurs in prev.mode normally has the function of delineating the area of reference to which the state or the action denoted by the verb is applied.[15] This can be illustrated by the nouns *indhŏ* (n.m.pl.) 'eyes', *lacăg* (n.f.) 'money', *hădal* (n.m.) 'speech', 'words' and *qŏsol* (n.m.) 'laughter' when they occur in prev.mode and are followed by forms of the verbs *bĕel* (v.Z) 'to cease to possess' and *badăn* (v.AN†) (in this context) 'to have a large quantity of', 'to abound in'.

> *Wŭu indhŏ beelay.*
>
> 'He (!)became blind(!).' Lit. 'He (!)ceased to possess(!) eyes.'

> *Wuu lacăg beelay.*
>
> 'He (!)was left with no(!) money at all.' Lit. 'He (!)ceased to possess(!) money.'

> *Wuu hădal badnaa.*
>
> 'He (!)was talkative(!).'

> *Wuu qŏsol badnaa.*
>
> 'He (!)was full of(!) laughter.'

The facts described above make it clear that the concept of ICC could not be equated with that of a sentence nucleus on account of the difficulties which would arise in establishing the "irreducible minimum" content of sentences containing a lex.int.phr. or a noun in prev.mode.

Section X
ABSENCE OF INDICATORS

A sentence has no indicator under the following conditions:

(i)   when its main verb belongs to any paradigm listed in column 0 in Table II, Section IV;

(ii) when its main verb belongs to the paradigm given in column 6 in Table II, Section IV, and when, at the same time, the sentence is a proverb or an expression using obviously archaic diction, e.g. *Nooli kulantee.* 'A person who is alive is likely to meet [another person who is alive].', where *kulantee* 'is likely to meet' is a V6 form;

(iii) when it contains the inter.w.IV or the inter.w.VII;

(iv) when its main verb consists of an inf. followed by a form of the auxiliary verb *măayŏ* (BE 53: 66); note that Moreno's materials suggest that this auxiliary verb is a compound in which the first component is *ma-!* (ind.) and the second is the verb *hăy* (v.IN) 'to hold', 'to continue [to do something]' (MO 55: 270).

The absence of an indicator can be an optional alternative to the presence of *băa* (*ayăa, yăa*) when the N1 or N5 unit which precedes it consists of an inter.def. or nom.aggr.II, e.g.

> *Kĕe băa la cunaa?*
>
> 'Which one does one eat?'

> *Kĕe la cunaa?*
>
> (The same meaning as above.)

---

[15]Sometimes a noun of this type in prev.mode can be replaced by a nom.aggr.I composed of the noun + def.art.gen (form A). The conditions under which this happens require further, extensive investigation.

Awrkĝe bằa cunằ?

'Which he-camel eats it?'

Awrkĝe cunằ?

(The same meaning as above.)

In addition, indicators may be absent in unfinished sentences or when the speaker changes his mind in the middle of the sentence and begins another construction. They are also absent in elliptical sentences, such as short answers to questions, e.g. *Bịyŏ.* 'Water.', in answer to the question *Maxằad dǫonaysaa?* 'What do you want?' Particularly frequent is the elliptical question *Magacằa?* 'Your name?'

Similarly, indicators may be absent in short ejaculatory expressions, e.g. *Yằab!* 'How amazing!', *Wẹgêr!* 'Beware!'

For a further discussion of the absence of indicators readers are referred to HE 65. Of particular importance are the observations made in that article which concern the absence of *bằa* in interrogative sentences (HE 65: 128).

Section XI

RELEVANCE OF THE STUDY OF INDICATOR CENTRED CORES TO OTHER AREAS OF SOMALI SYNTAX

The study of ICCs, as I hope has been demonstrated, is essential for our understanding of the rôles of indicators. It can also be relevant to the description of other aspects of Somali syntax, since it provides a readily recognizable framework of reference applicable to the majority of sentences. In this section I shall endeavour to show how this framework of reference can be employed to handle some specific problems.

It is a puzzling characteristic of Somali that in a sentence which contains a subj.pron. as the subject of the verb another item can occur to which that subj.pron. refers. Both the subj.pron. and the additional item stand in concord with the same verb, e.g.

Nĩnkani ằwr bǔu keenay.

'This man brought (!)a he-camel(!).'

In this sentence both *nĩnkani* 'this man' and *uu* (in *bǔu* which = *bằa* + *uu*) 'he' stand in concord with the verbal form *keenay* 'brought', so that the literal translation could be 'This man he brought (!)a he-camel(!).'

The additional subject can consist of any of the items listed under N2 in Table I, Section IV, with the only exception of the impers.pron. The position of such an item in the sentence depends on the context of the subj.pron. Two contexts have to be recognized:

(i) when the subj.pron. occurs as N2^C, as part of an ICC, and

(ii) when the subj.pron. occurs in the position marked [X] in the ICCs listed below:

    ma-! [X] !V1!

    ma-! [X] !V4!

    ma-! [X] !V5!

    soo-! *ma-!* [X] !V5!

    waa-! [X] !V1!

The additional subject can occur:

(a) Either before the first or after the last component of the ICC when the subj.pron. is either in context (i) or (ii)

(b)   between the only or the last ind. and the V unit when the subj.pron. is in context (i).

Examples:

(a)   (i)   *Nínkani àwr bùu keenay.*

'This man brought (!)a he-camel(!).' (Note that *bùu = bàa + uu.*)

Àwr bùu keenay nínkani.

(The same meaning.)

(a)   (ii)   *Nínkani mú uu ḳẹenín.*

'This man (!)did not bring(!) it (etc.).' (Note that *mú uu = mã uu.*)

Mú uu ḳẹenín nínkani.

(The same meaning.)

(b)   (i)   *Àwr bùu ninkani keenay.*

'This man brought (!)a he-camel(!).'

It should be noted that the words "before," "after" and "between" used in the above formulation delineate limits but do not imply contiguity. The positions of the items under discussion in relation to other items which can occur in the sentence are subject to various rules such as, for example, those given in AN 60: 101 or ZH 66: 143-166.

ICCs can also provide a framework for exclusion rules of various kinds. Thus for example we can state that no repetition of the subject of the verb, whatever this subject may be, can occur if the ICC contains $!N5^C!$, $!N6^C!$ or $!N7^C!$.

Certain ICCs can serve as a useful reference framework in the description of dependent verbal clauses which form part of nom.cls. Every positive dependent verbal clause which is convergent i.e. has a headword which stands in concord with its verb, can be described by reference to the ICC represented by $!N5^C!$ *bàa* $V3^C$.

A nom.cl. containing a convergent dependent verbal clause can be derived from a sentence the ICC of which is $!N5^C!$ *bàa* $V3^C$ provided that N5 is one of the following items: dem., n., card.num., appr.num., unsp.num. or nom.aggr.I.

This can be achieved by:

(a)   deleting the ind. *bàa,* and

(b)   substituting V3 by a corresponding form of a cvg. (convergent) or dep.inf. paradigm. Note that the distribution of the A and B forms of convergent paradigms is determined by the same factors as those which are involved in the declensions of nouns (see Section V of this article and AN 68: 2-4).

Examples:

Rág bàa keená.

'(!)Men(!) bring it (etc.).'

rág keená

'men who bring it (etc.)'

Rággàa keená.

'(!)The men(!) bring it (etc.).', where *rággàa = rágga* 'the men' + *bàa*

rágga keená

'the men who bring it (etc.)'

Rágga keená ú yèedh!

'Call the men who bring it (etc.)!'

Rágga keenaa má jgogaan?

'(!)Are(!) the men who bring it (etc.) (!)present(!)?'

A similar procedure can be applied to a nom.cl. which contains a divergent dependent verbal clause, i.e. a clause the headword of which does not stand in concord with its verb. A nom. cl. of this kind can be derived from a sentence in which the ICC is $!N1!$ *bàa* $N2^C$ $V1^C$, provided that the N1 is one of the items enumerated in the formulation relating to N5 given above.

The rules of derivation consist of:

(a) deleting the ind. *bàa*, and

(b) substituting V1 by a corresponding form of a dvg. (divergent) or dep.inf. paradigm. The distribution of the A and B form of dvg. paradigms is determined by the same factors as the case of cvg. paradigms.

Examples:

Hjlib bùu keenaa.

'He brings (!)meat(!).'

hjlib uu keenó

'meat which he brings'

Hjlibkùu keenaa.

'He brings (!)the meat(!).', where *hjlibkùu* = *hjlibka* 'the meat' + *uu* 'he'

hjlibkuu keenó

'the meat which he brings', where *hjlibkuu* = *hjlibka* 'the meat' + *uu* 'he'

Hjlibkuu keenó cún!

'Eat the meat which he brings!'

Hjlibkuu keenaa waa qáali.

'The meat which he brings is (!)an expensive commodity(!).'

Nom.cls. containing negative dependent verbal clauses can be derived from sentences in which the ICC is either $!N5^C!$ *bàa aan·* $V2^C$ or $!N1!$ *bàa aan·* $N2^C$ $V2^C$ by similar procedures.

Section XII

EXAMPLES OF INDICATOR CENTRED CORES DRAWN FROM WIDER CONTEXTS

The aim of this section is to illustrate the formulations concerning ICCs by examples drawn from wider contexts such as plays, narratives, newspaper articles and proverbs.

Each example is provided with extensive annotations which are designed to enable the reader not familiar with Somali to account for each component of the sentence and for all the important relationships between these components. The text of each example is provided with a translation in which, unlike in the previous examples, emphasis is not marked by means of exclamation marks in brackets. It is left to the reader to arrive at the information by referring to the analyses of the ICCs provided at the end of each group of annotations. After the translation an indication of the source is given and a brief account of the context from which the example was taken, with the view of giving a clear delineation of its meaning.

Lexical information is provided for each word in every example. Representative forms of nouns and verbs are given first and are followed by explanations concerning the forms which actually occur in the text. The same procedure is applied to all other word classes and it is to be assumed that the forms given in the lists in Section II are their representative forms. If the representative form of a word is identical with its form in the text the sign - - - is used in the annotation. For all abbreviations used in the annotations see Sections II-V.

Furthermore, all aggregates and clusters (see Section III) are accounted for in the annotations. I am aware of the fact that such information is often only of marginal relevance to the main theme of this article but I have been reluctant to leave it out since it contains some points of interest which may inspire some readers to undertake further research and to embark on further theoretical speculation. This would be particularly welcome in the areas of grammar to which I have applied the concepts of setting, configuration and case. I hope that perhaps other researchers who may be attracted to handle these challenging problems in Somali will produce a set of neater formulations than those available at present.

Each example is preceded by a figure which refers to the index in Section XIII arranged according to the ICCs which the annotated examples illustrate. It should be noted that the examples given in this section do not cover the whole range of ICCs. The annotated texts in MJ 56 may serve as further illustrations, even though the annotations given there do not include analyses of ICCs.

/1/ *Doqôn milantáy iyo gǧesi mallâafsi bartâa miidaani kǎ dhêx dhacdaa.*

'A mighty battle [usually] breaks out between simple people who have become submissive and a bold man who has grown accustomed to bullying [them].' Proverb. This proverb asserts that the meek if driven beyond the limits of their endurance become formidable fighters against their oppressors.

doqôn.......bartâa = doqôn.......bartáy + bǎa

doqôn.......bartáy (nom.cl./smp.stg., clo.cf.) 'simple people who have become submissive and a bold man who has grown accustomed to bullying [them]'

doqôn milantáy (nom.cl./intg.stg., cct.cfg.) 'simple people who have become submissive'

dôqon (n.m.) 'a simple person', 'a fool'; *doqôn* (n.f. sub-pl.) 'simple people', 'fools'; - - - (intg.stg., cct.cfg.)

mîlan (v.Z) 'to melt', 'to become weak', 'to become submissive'; *milantáy* (3sg.f.past gen.cvg.A)

iyo⸴ (conj.) 'and'; *iyo* (pos.var.)

gǧesi.......bartáy (nom.cl./intg.stg., clo.cfg.) 'a bold man who has grown accustomed to bullying [them]'

gǧesi (n.m.) 'a brave man', 'a bold man'; - - - (intg.stg., cct.cfg.)

mallâafsi (n.m.) 'bullying', 'intimidation'; - - - (intg.stg., ope.cfg., case A)

barô (v.AN) 'to learn', 'to grow accustomed to'; *bartáy* (3sg.m.past gen.cvg.A)

bǎa (ind.)

miidâan (n.f.) 'a large open area', 'a large battlefield', 'a mighty battle'; *miidaani* (smp.stg., ope.cfg. case B)

ka⸴ (prep.ptc.) 'in', 'at'; *kǎ* (pos.var.)

dhêx (n.f.) '[the] middle [part of something]'; - - - (smp.stg., ope.cfg., case A);
    note that *dhêx* occurs here in prev.mode and has the meaning 'between'

dhâc (v.Z) 'to fall', 'to occur', 'to break out'; *dhacdaa* (3sg.f.pres.gen.ext.)

ICC = !N1! *bàa* N2^C V1^C
    N1 = *doqôn.......bartây*
    N2 = *miidaani*
    V1 = *dhacdaa*

/2/   *Gôormàan imaaddaa?*

'When shall I come?' AL 66: 10. The character in the play asks the girl whom he is
courting when he could visit her again. At this point he has to leave her in a hurry
because of the unexpected arrival of her father, who disapproves of him, in the
courtyard of the house.

gôormàan = gôorma + bàa + aan

gôorma (inter.w.I) 'when?'; cf. *gôor* (n.f.) 'time'

bàa (ind.)

aan (1sg.subj.pron.)

yimi (v.STR) 'to come'; *imaaddaa* (1sg.pres.gen.ext.); note that the forms of the pres.
    gen.ext. prardigm frequently convey future time reference when they are used in
    questions.

ICC = !N1! *bàa* N2^C V1^C
    N1 = *gôorma*
    N2 = *aan*
    V1 = *imaaddaa*

/3/   *Ma sàasàan kû idhaahaa?*

'Shall I say [just] that to him?' AN and MJ 66: 37. In this traditional story a
traveller is given an incomprehensible message to someone in a distant village. He is
astonished by the wording and the brevity of the message and puts this question to
the sender to confirm that he wants it to be transmitted in that form. The traveller
does not know that the message is in a kind of secret code.

ma! (ind.); *ma* (pos.var.)

sàasàan = sidaasàan = sidâas bàan

sidâas (nom.aggr.I/smp.stg., clo.cfg.), (lit. 'that way' but note that this nom.aggr.
    refers to the contents of the message and not to the way in which it should be
    delivered) = *si + tâas*

si (n.f.) 'way', 'manner'

tâas (dem.f.) 'that'; - - - (form A)

bàan = bàa + aan

bàa (ind.)

aan (1sg.subj.pron.)

ku! (prep.ptc.) 'to'; *kû* (pos.var.)

yidhi (v.STR) 'to say'; *idhaahaa* or *idhaahdaa* (1sg.pres.gen.ext.); note that the forms
    of the pres.gen.ext. paradigm frequently convey future time reference when they
    are used in questions.

ICC = ma⁼ ⌐N1⌐ bàa N2^C V1^C
N1 = *sídáas*
N2 = *aan*
V1 = *idhaahaa*

/4/   *Warshadáynta iyo kallúunsigu wáxay noqón doonaan xubnó wę̂yn oo dhaqaalêhe̲enna tiirín doona.*

'Industrialization and fishing will become large sectors which will give support to our economy.' JA 74: 26 June, 2. A statement in an article about the importance of these two sectors of Somali economy.

warshadáynta iyo kallúunsigu (nom.cl./smp.stg., ope.cfg., case B)

warshadáynta (nom.aggr.I/intg.stg., cct.cfg.) = *warshadáyn* + *ta*

warshadáyn or *warshadéyn* (n.f.) 'industrialization'; cf. *warshád* (n.f.) 'factory' and *warshadée* (v.AYN) 'to industrialize'

ta (def.art.gen.f.); - - - (form A)

iyo⁼ (conj.) 'and'; *iyo* (pos.var.)

kallúunsigu (nom.aggr.I/intg.stg., ope.cfg., case B) = *kallúunsi* + *ku*

kallúunsi (n.m.) 'fishing'; cf. *kallúun* (n.m.) 'fish'

ka (def.art.gen.m.); *ku* (form B)

wáxay = *wáxa ay*

wáxa (ind.)

ay (3pl.subj.pron.) 'they' (i.e. 'industrialization and fishing')

noqó (v.ON) 'to become'; *noqón* (inf.)

dòon (v.Z) an auxiliary verb used here with the inf. form *noqón*, conveying future time reference; *doonaan* (3p.pres.gen.ext.)

xubnó.......dooná (nom.cl./smp.stg., neu.cfg.) lit. 'sectors which are large and which will give support to our economy'

xubín (n.f.) 'a joint [of a limb]', 'member', 'sector'; *xubnŏ* (n.m.pl.); *xubnó* (intg. stg., cct.cfg.)

wę̂yn (v.Z+) 'to be large'; - - - (pres.cvg.A)

oo⁼ (conj.) 'and'; *oo* (pos.var.)

dhaqaalêhe̲enna (nom.aggr.I/intg.stg., ope.cfg. case A = *dhaqáale* + *ke̲en⁼* + *ka*

dhaqáale (n.m.) 'economy', 'thrift'

ke̲en⁼ (1pl.incl.poss.def.m.) 'our'

ka (def.art.gen.m.); - - - (form A)

tiiri (v.IN) 'to give support to', 'to prop', *tiirín* (inf. dep.)

dòon (v.Z) an auxiliary verb used here with the inf. form *tiirín*, conveying future time reference; *dooná* (3pl.pres.gen.cvg.A)

ICC = *wáxa* N2^C V1^C ⌐N4⌐
N2 = *ay*
V1 = *noqón doonaan*
N4 = *xubnó.......dooná*

/5/   *Márkáa ma wáxaad do̲onaysaa ínaan fikrád hálkáa káa siiyó?*

'Then do you want me to give you an opinion about that point?', lit. 'Then do you want that I should give you an opinion about that point?' HA 66: 3. A character in the play puts this question to a friend who has come to seek his advice on how to elope with a girl at night from her father's house. The friend states that the girl's father is kept awake by a chronic cough and that he keeps a watch dog.

márkáa (nom.aggr.I/smp.stg.ope.cfg., case A) 'then', 'in that case'= már + káa

már (n.m.) 'time', 'point in time'

káa (dem.m.); - - - (form A)

ma⁻ (ind.); ma (pos.var.)

wáxaad = wáxa aad

wáxa (ind.)

aad (2sg.subj.pron.)

dǒon (v.Z) 'to want', 'to seek'; dǒonaysaa or dǒoneysaa (2sg.pres.cnt.ext.)

ínaan.......siiyó (para-nom.cl.I/smp.stg., neu.cfg.) 'that I should give you an opinion about that point'

ínaan = ín + aan

ín (decl.ptc.) 'that'

aan (1sg.subj.pron.)

fikrád (n.f.) 'opinion', 'thought', 'idea'; - - - (intg.stg., ope.cfg., case A)

hálkáa (nom.aggr.I/intg.stg., ope.cfg., case A) = hál + káa

hál (n.m.) 'a point [in a discussion]'

káa (dem.m.); - - - (form A)

káa = ku + ka⁻

ku (2sg.obj.pron.I)

ka⁻ (prep.ptc.) 'about', 'concerning'

sii (v.IN) 'to give'; siiyó (1sg.pres.gen.dvg.A)

ICC = ma⁻ wáxa N2^C V1^C !N4!
    N2 = aad
    V1 = dǒonaysaa
    N4 = ínaan.......siiyó

/6/ Arládáasna dameeráa iyo ẹyda iyo baqáalku waa kú qáali, maxáa yeeláy gẹel báanay laháyn.

'And in that country donkeys, dogs and mules are an expensive commodity because they do not have camels.' MU 56: 48. From a traditional adventure story concerning Cigaal Bowkax, a well known Somali traveller and wit who once went to South Africa. He was astonished by the high price of domestic animals and attributed it to the total absence of camels which he had observed. By 'they' are meant the inhabitants of the country.

arládáasna = arládáas na

arládáas (nom.aggr.I/smp.stg., ope.cfg., case A) = árlo + táas

árlo (n.f.) 'country'

táas (dem.f.) 'that'; - - - (form A)

na⁻ (conj.) 'and'; na (pos.var.)

dameeráa.......baqáalku (nom.cl./smp.stg., ope.cfg., case B) 'donkeys, dogs and mules'

dameeráa = dameeráha

dameeráha (nom.aggr.I/intg.stg., cct.cfg.) = dameerǒ + ka

damêer (n.f.) 'a she-donkey'; dameerŏ (n.m.plur.) 'she-donkeys' or 'donkeys of both
      sexes'; cf. damêer (n.m.) 'a he-donkey', dameerrŏ (n.f.pl.) 'he-donkeys'

ka (def.art.gen.m.); - - - (form A)

iyo⁻' (conj.) 'and'; iyo (pos.var.)

ệyda (nom.aggr.I/intg.stg., cct.cfg.) = ệy + ta

ệy (n.m.) 'a dog'; ệy (n.f.sub-pl.) 'dogs'

ta (def.art.gen.f.); - - - (form A)

iyo⁻' (conj.) 'and'; iyo (pos.var.)

baqâalku (nom.aggr.I/intg.stg., ope.cfg., case B) = baqâal + ku

baqâal (n.m.coll.) 'mules'

ka (def.art.gen.m.); kú (form B)

waa⁻' (ind.); waa (pos.var.)

ku⁻' (prep.ptc.) 'in'; ku (pos.var.)

qâali (n.m.) 'an expensive commodity', 'high price'; - - - (smp.stg., neu.cfg.)

maxâa = maxây + bâa

maxây (inter.w.II):: bâa (ind.).:. yeelây (3sg.m.past gen.res. of yêel, v.Z), (lex.int.
      phr.) 'because'

maxây (inter.w.II) component of the above lex.int.phr.; note that in other contexts it
      means 'what?'

bâa (ind.) component of the above lex.int.phr.

yêel (v.Z) component of the above lex.int.phr.; note that in other contexts it means
      'to do' or 'to accept'

gệel (n.m.coll.) 'camels'; - - - (smp.stg., clo.cfg.)

bâanay = bâa + aan⁻' + ay

bâa (ind.)

aan⁻' (neg.ptc.)

ay (3pl.subj.pron.)

lêh or lê (v.Z†) 'to have'; lahâyn (neg.pres.-past.)

Arlâdâasna.......lahâyn, note that this example consists of three sentences:

(1)   Arlâdâasna.......qâali.

(2)   Maxâa yeelây.

(3)   Gệel.......lahâyn.

ICC (1) = waa⁻' !N8!
          N8 = qâali

ICC (2) = !N5ᶜ! bâa V3ᶜ
          N5 = maxây
          V3 = yeelây

ICC (3) = !N1! bâa aan⁻' N2ᶜ V2ᶜ
          N1 = gệel
          N2 = ay
          V2 = lahâyn   .

/7/   Wâxâan shaki kú jirin haddii sí wacân lôo ururiyŏ xâbâgta dâlka lagâ helô in lacâg
      farabadân loogâ hệli doonô tâasôo kaalin wệyn kâ gệysân doontâ horumarînta dhaqaalâha.

'There is no doubt that if one collects in a proper way the gum which one finds in the
country one will get much money from it for [the country], [it being] that which will
bring great help to the development of the economy.' JA 74: 26 June, 3. From an article
about the cultivation of gum in Somalia.

wáxáan = *wáxa* + *aan*⁻

wáxa (ind.)

aan⁻ (neg.ptc.)

shāki (n.m.) 'doubt'; *shaki* (smp.stg., ope.cfg., case B)

ku⁻ (prep.ptc.) 'in'; *kú* (pos.var.)

jĭr (v.Z) 'to be', 'to exist'; *jĭrín* (neg.pres.-past gen.)

haddíi.......*helô* (nom.cl./smp.stg., ope.cfg. case A) 'if one collects in a proper way
     the gum which one finds in the country'

haddíi (nom.aggr.I/intg.stg., cct.cfg.) 'if', [under] the condition [that]' = *had* + *tíi*

had (n.f.) 'condition', 'circumstance'; note that the occurrence of this word is limited
     to nom.cl., in which it functions as the headword of a divergent dependent verbal
     clause; note also that it has an irregular accentual pattern for a sg.fem.noun not
     ending in -*o* (see AN 64a: 32-33); *had* should not be confused with *hád* (n.f.) 'time',
     'present time'.

tíi (def.art.rem.f.); - - - (form A)

sí wacán (nom.cl./intg.stg., ope.cfg., case A) lit. 'a way which is proper'

sí (n.f.) 'way', 'manner'; - - - (intg.stg., cct.cfg.)

wacán (v.AN†) 'to be proper', 'to be good'; - - - (pres.cvg.A)

lôo = *la* + *u*⁻

la (impers.pron.) 'someone', 'one', 'people'

u⁻ (prep.ptc.) 'in', 'according to'

urúri (v.IN) 'to collect', 'to gather'; *ururiyô* (3sg.m.pres.gen.dvg.A)

xabágta.......*helô* (nom.cl./intg.stg., ope.cfg., case A) 'the gum which one finds in
     the country'

xabágta (nom.aggr.I/intg.stg., cct.cfg.) = *xabág* + *ta*

xabág (n.f.) 'gum'

ta (def.art.gen.f.); - - - (form A)

dálka (nom.aggr.I/intg.stg., ope.cfg., case A) = *dál* + *ka*

dál (n.m.) 'country'

ka (def.art.gen.m.); - - - (form A)

lagá = *la* + *ka*⁻

la (impers.pron.) 'someone', 'one', 'people'

ka⁻ (prep.ptc.) 'in', 'from'

hél (v.Z) 'to find'; *helô* (3sg.m.pres.gen.dvg.A)

in.......*doonô* (para-nom.cl.I/smp.stg., neu.cfg.) 'that one will get much money from
     it for [the country]'

in (decl.ptc.) 'that'

lacág farabadán (nom.cl./intg.stg., ope.cfg., case A) lit. 'money which is large in
     number'

lacág (n.f.) 'money'; - - - (intg.stg., cct.cfg.)

farabadắn = *farǎ badắn* = *farǒ badắn*

fắr (n.f.) 'a finger'; *farǒ* (n.m.pl.) 'fingers'; - - - (intg.stg., ope.cfg., case A)

badắn (v.AN†) 1. when preceded by a n. or a nom.aggr.I which is not its subject: 'to
    have a large number or quantity of what is denoted by that n. or nom.aggr.'',
    2. in all other contexts: 'to be large in number or quantity'; - - - (pres.cvg.A)

farǒ (n.m.pl.).:. *badắn* (v.AN), (lex.int.phr.) 'to be numerous', lit.(?) 'to have a
    large number of fingers'

loogắ = *la* + *u⌐* + *ka⌐*

la (impers.pron.) 'someone', 'one', 'people'

u⌐ (prep.ptc.) 'to', 'for'

ka⌐ (prep.ptc.) 'in', 'from'

hễl (v.Z) 'to find'; *hễli* (inf.dep.)

dŏon (v.Z) an auxiliary verb used here with the inf.dep. form *hễli*, conveying future
    time reference; *doonŏ* (3sg.m.pres.gen.dvg.A)

tắasŏo.......dhaqaalắha (nom.cl./smp.stg., ope.cfg., case A) '[it being] that which will
    give great help to the development of the economy'; note that *tắas* (dem.f.) when
    it is linked by *oo⌐* (conj.) to the verbal clause dependent on it, has a semantic
    function similar to that of an absolute clause of attendant circumstance in English.

tắasŏo = *tắas* + *oo⌐*

tắas (dem.f.) 'that'

oo⌐ (conj.) 'and', 'while'; *ŏo* (pos.var.), see MJ 56: 77, Note 7a.

kaalĭn wễyn (nom.cl./intg.stg., ope.cfg., case A) lit. 'help which is great'

kaalĭn (n.f.) 'help', 'participating rôle', 'place', 'position'; - - - (intg.stg.,
    cct.cfg.)

wễyn (v.Z†) 'to be great', 'to be big'; - - - (pres.cvg.A)

ka⌐ (prep.ptc.) 'in', 'to'; *kắ* (pos.var.)

geysŏ (v.IN/SAN) 'to bring for oneself (i.e. for one's own benefit)', 'to bring about',
    'to cause'; *geysắn* (inf.dep.)

dŏon (v.Z) an auxiliary verb used here with the inf.dep. form *geysắn*, conveying future
    time reference; *doontắ* (3sg.f.pres.gen.cvg.A)

horumarĭnta dhaqaalắha (nom.cl./intg.stg., ope.cfg., case A) 'the development of the
    economy'

horumarĭnta (nom.aggr.I/intg.stg., cct.cfg.) = *horumarĭn* + *ta*

horumarĭn (n.f.) 'development', 'progress', cf. *horễ* (adv.n.I) 'forward', 'before', *u⌐*
    (prep.ptc.) 'to' and *mắri* (v.IN) 'to cause to pass'

ta (def.art.gen.f.); - - - (form A)

dhaqaalắha (nom.aggr.I/sub.gnt.stg., ope.cfg., case A) = *dhaqắale* + *ka*

dhaqắale (n.m.) 'economy', 'thrift'

ka (def.art.gen.m.); - - - (form A)

ICC = *wắxa aan⌐* N2^C V2^C !N4!
    N2 = *shaki*
    V2 = *jirĭn*
    N4 = *in.......doonŏ*

/8/   *Qawaanĭinta cắynkắas ắh wắxaanay sĭ wạnaagsắn ugŭ muuqắn ama danắyn dắdka aan hắdalka
      kắ fiirsắn ee dắntǫoduba tahắy ĭn la gartŏ wắxay ŭ jeedāan.*

'[As for] the rules which are of that kind, they are not clearly apparent to or do not interest the people who do not reflect upon speech and whose concern is merely that one should understand what they mean.' AX 74: 5. From an article about the importance of linguistic research. The rules in question are those of grammar.

qawaaníinta.......âh (nom.cl./smp.stg., ope.cfg., case A) lit. 'the rules which are that kind'; note that in this context the nom.cl. could also occur in case B since it could stand in concord with the main verb. In case B the form *âh* would be replaced by *ahi* or *ihi*.

qawaaníinta (nom.aggr.I/intg.stg., cct.cfg.) = *qawaaníin* + *ta*

qaynùun (n.m.) 'rule', 'law'; *qawaaníin* (n.f.sub-pl.) 'rules', 'laws'

ta (def.art.gen.f.); - - - (form A)

câynkâas (nom.aggr.I/intg.stg., ope.cfg., case A) = *câyn* + *kâas*

câyn (n.m.) 'kind', 'type'

kâas (dem.m.) 'that'; - - - (form A)

yₐhay (v.STR) 'to be', 'to belong to'; *âh* (pres.cvg.A); note that the final *h* in *âh* is not pronounced in this context but is written here in conformity with the usage of the Somali national orthography

wâxaanay = *wâxa* + *aan⁻* + *ay*

wâxa (ind.)

aan⁻ (neg.ptc.)

ay (3pl.subj.pron.)

sí wₐnaagsân (nom.cl./smp.stg., ope.cfg., case A) lit. 'a way which is good', translated here as 'clearly'

sí (n.f.) 'way', 'manner'; - - - (intg.stg., cct.cfg.)

wₐnaagsân (v.SAN†) 'to be good'; - - - (pres.cvg.A)

ugû = *u⁻* + *u⁻*

u⁻ (prep.ptc.) refers here to *sí wₐnaagsân* and could be rendered as 'in': *sí wₐnaagsân .:. u⁻* 'in a good way'

u⁻ (prep.ptc.) 'to'; this second prep.ptc. refers to *dâdka.......jₑedâan*

muuqô (v.AN) 'to be visible', 'to be apparent'; *muuqân* (neg.pres.-past gen.)

ama⁻ or *amma⁻* (conj.) 'or'

danêe (v.AYN) 'to interest', 'to concern', 'to be of advantage to'; *danâyn* or *danêyn* (neg.pres.-past gen.)

dâdka.......jₑedâan (nom.cl./smp.stg., neu.cfg.) 'the people who do not reflect upon speech and whose concern is merely that one should understand what they mean'

dâdka (nom.aggr.I/intg.stg., cct.cfg.) = *dâd* + *ka*

dâd (n.m.coll.) 'people'

ka (def.art.gen.m.); - - - (form A)

aan.......fiirsân, a verbal clause dependent on *dâdka* as its headword, 'who do not reflect on speech'

aan⁻ (neg.ptc.)

hâdalka (nom.aggr.I/intg.stg., ope.cfg., case A) = *hâdal* + *ka*

hâdal (n.m.) 'speech', 'words'

ka (def.art.gen.m.); - - - (form A)

ka⁼ (prep.ptc.) 'upon', 'about'; *kā* (pos.var.)

fiirsô (v.SAN) 'to reflect', 'to think', 'to consider carefully'; *fiirsán* (neg.pres.-
     past gen.dep.A)

ee⁼ or *e⁼* (conj.) 'and'; *ee* (pos.var.)

dãntǫoduba.......jǫedãan, another verbal clause dependent on *dãdka* as its headword,
     'whose concern is merely that one should understand what they mean'

dãntǫoduba = dãntǫodu ba⁼

dãntǫodu (nom.aggr.I/intg.stg., ope.cfg., case B) = *dãn + tǫod⁼ + tu*

dãn (n.f.) 'concern', 'interest'

tǫod⁼ (3pl.poss.def.f.) 'their'; this poss.def. refers to *dãdka*

ta (def.art.gen.f.); *tu* (form B)

ba⁼ (distr.ptc.) 'altogether', 'merely', *ba* (pos.var.)

yǫhay (v.STR) 'to be', 'to consist of'; *tahãy* (3sg.f.pres.dvg.A)

ĩn.......jǫedãan (para-nom.cl.I/intg.stg., ope.cfg. case A) 'that one should understand
     what they mean'

ĩn (decl.ptc.) 'that'

la (impers.pron.) 'someone', 'one', 'people'

garô (v.AN) 'to understand', 'to recognize'; *gartô* (3sg.m.pres.gen.dvg.A)

wãxay ũ jǫedãan (nom.cl./intg.stg., ope.cfg., case A) lit. 'the thing which they mean'

wãxay = wãxa ay

wãxa (nom.aggr.I/intg.stg., cct.cfg.) = *wãx + ka*

wãx (n.m.) 'a thing', 'things'

ka (def.art.gen.m.); - - - (form A)

ay (3pl.subj.pron.)

u⁼ (prep.ptc.) .:. *jǫed* (v.Z), (lex.int.phr.) 'to mean', 'to intend'

u⁼ (prep.ptc.) component of the above lex.int.phr., *ũ* (pos.var.)

jǫed (v.Z) component of the above lex.int.phr., *jǫedãan* (3pl.pres.gen.dvg.A); note that
     outside this lex.int.phr. this verb usually means 'to face [in a particular
     direction]'

ICC = *wãxa aan⁼* N2^C V2^C ⁼N4⁼
    N2 = *ay* (within *wãxaanay*)
    V2 = *muuqãn* or *danãyn*
    N4 = *dãdka.......jǫedãan*

/9/   *Sirmaqabê Ãllãw sǫhan tagá.*

'God goes on reconnaissance for the man who has no evil secrets.' Proverb. This
proverb is used when commenting on an innocent person's triumph when an attempt to harm
him fails or false or hasty accusations are proved to be unfounded.

   sirmaqábe (n.m.) 'a man who has no evil secrets', this is an imaginary descriptive name;
      cf. *sir* (n.f.) 'secret', 'evil secret', *ma⁼* (ind.), *qãb* (v.Z) 'to have' and the
      suffix -*e* which usually means 'the performer of the action described by the root'
      of the related verb', *sirmaqabê* (smp.stg., ope.cfg., case A)

Ãllãw = Ãlle + bãa + u⁼

Ãlle or *Ãlla* (n.m.) 'God'; *Ãlle* (smp.stg., clo.cfg.)

bǎa (ind.)

u⊥ (prep.ptc.) 'for'

sǎhan (n.m.) 'a reconnaissance which nomadic pastoralists send out to look for an area which has good grazing and water and is free from danger', 'the activities of such a reconnaissance'; - - - (smp.stg.ope.cfg., case A), used here in prev.mode, hence the translation 'on reconnaissance'

tǎg (v.Z) 'to go'; *tagǎ* (3sg.m.pres.gen.res.)

$$ICC = \,!N5^C\,!\; b\check{a}a\; V3^C$$
$$N5 = \hat{A}lle$$
$$V3 = tag\check{a}$$

/10/ *Maxǎa adǎg?*

'What is difficult [about it]?' HA 66: 2. This question is put by a character in the play to his friend who plans an elopement and complains about the difficulties which could arise because of the watch dog kept by the girl's father.

maxǎa = maxǎy + bǎa

maxǎy (inter.w.II) 'what?'

bǎa (ind.)

adǎg (v.Z†) 'to be hard', 'to be difficult'; - - - (pres.res.)

$$ICC = \,!N5^C\,!\; b\check{a}a\; V3^C$$
$$N5 = max\check{a}y$$
$$V3 = ad\check{a}g$$

/11/ *Ma dhǐrtǎa ina shěegaysǎ?*

'Will the trees report us?' AL 67: 2. This question is addressed by one of the thieves in the play to a new associate who is reluctant to admit what his real name is, even though the conversation is conducted in an isolated spot in the country.

ma⊥ (ind.); *ma* (pos.var.)

dhǐrtǎa = dhǐrta + bǎa

dhǐrta (nom.aggr.I/smp.stg., clo.cfg.) = *dhǐr + ta*

dhǐr (n.f.) 'trees', 'bushes'

ta (def.art.gen.f.); - - - (form A)

bǎa (ind.)

ina (1pl.incl.obj.pron.I) 'us'

shěeg (v.Z) 'to report', 'to tell'; *shěegaysǎ* or *shěegeysǎ* (3sg.f.pres.cnt.res.)

$$ICC = ma^{\perp}\; !N6^C\,!\; b\check{a}a\; V3^C$$
$$N6 = dh\check{i}rta$$
$$V3 = sh\check{e}egays\check{a}$$

/12/ *Wǎxaan ku lěeÿahay, cǐd miyǎa kulǎ socotǎy?*

'I say, are you accompanied by anyone?', lit. 'I say to you, "Has a person walked with you?"' AL 66: 25. This question is put by a character in the play to a girl in a night club in the hope that she is free.

wâxaan = *wâxa* + *aan*

wâxa (ind.)

aan (1sg.subj.pron.)

ku (2sg.obj.pron.I)

lêh or *lê* (v.Z†) 'to be saying [something]', 'to be in the process of saying [something]';
     lêeÿahay (1sg.pres.ext.)

cíd.......*socotây* (quot.p./smp.stg., ope.cfg., case A) 'has a person walked with you?'

cíd (n.f.) 'people', 'persons', 'a person'; - - - (smp.stg., clo.cfg.)

míyàa (ind.)

kulâ = *ku* + *la⸗*

ku (2sg.obj.pron.I)

la⸗ (prep.ptc.) 'with'

socô (v.ON) 'to walk', 'to proceed'; *socotây* (3sg.f.past gen.res.)

Wâxaan.......*socotây*, note that this sentence contains a quot.p. which is a fully
     formed sentence itself.

ICC [of the whole sentence] = *wâxa* N2^C V1^C !N4!
     N2 = *aan*
     V1 = *leeÿahay*
     N4 = *cíd*.......*socotây*

ICC [of the quot.p.] = !N6^C! *míyàa* V3^C
     N6 = *cíd*
     V3 = *socotây*

/13/ *Wâxa jírá hâdal áʄkàaga kú xún oo áʄka walâalkâa kú wǫnaagsán.*

'There are words which are inappropriate in your own mouth but which are appropriate in
the mouth of your brother.' Proverb. This proverb refers to delicate matters which
are best handled by a brother or a friend rather than by the person directly concerned.

wâxa (ind.)

jír (v.Z) 'to be', 'to exist'; *jírá* (3sg.m.pres.gen.res.)

hâdal.......*wǫnaagsán* (nom.cl./smp.stg., neu.cfg.)

hâdal (n.m.) 'speech', 'words'; - - - (intg.stg. cct.cfg.)

áʄkàaga (nom.aggr.I/intg.stg., ope.cfg., case A) = *áʄ* + *kaa⸗* + *ka*

áʄ (n.m.) 'mouth', 'language'

kaa⸗ (2sg.poss.def.m.) 'your'

ka (def.art.gen.m.); - - - (form A)

ku⸗ (prep.ptc.) 'in'; *kú* (pos.var.)

xún (v.Z†) 'to be bad', 'to be inappropriate'; - - - (pres.cvg.A)

oo⸗ (conj.) 'and', 'but'; *oo* (pos.var.)

áʄka walâalkâa (nom.cl./intg.stg., ope.cfg., case A) 'the mouth of your brother'

áʄka (nom.aggr.I/intg.stg., cct.cfg.) = *áʄ* + *ka*

áʄ (n.m.) 'mouth', 'language'

ka (def.art.gen.m.); - - - (form A)

walåalkåa (nom.aggr.I/sub.gnt.stg./ope.cfg., case A) = *walåal* + *kaa⸗*

walåal (n.m.) 'brother'

kaa⸗ (2sg.poss.def.m.) 'your'

ku⸗ (prep.ptc.) 'in'; *kú* (pos.var.)

wǫnaagsån (v.SAN†) 'to be good', 'to be appropriate'; - - - (pres.cvg.A)

ICC = *wåxa* V3^C !N7^C!
    V3 = *jiråa*
    N7 = *håadal*.......*wǫnaagsån*

/14/ *Wållee cid båan idinkå saarin!*

'By God, no one can free you from it!' Lit. 'People do not free you from it!' AL 67: 12. These words are addressed to the thieves in the play who are caught in a trap-pit dug outside a house from which they were about to steal. The speaker is a member of a vigilante committee.

Wållee = *Wålle* + *e⸗*

Wålle (r.i.) 'By God!'; an interjection borrowed from Arabic

e⸗ or *ee⸗* (conj.) 'and'; this conj. links *Wålle* to the rest of the sentence

cid (n.f.) 'people'; - - - (smp.stg., clo.cfg.)

båan = *båa* + *aan⸗*

båa (ind.)

aan⸗ (neg.ptc.)

idinkå = *idin* + *ka⸗*

idin (2pl.obj.pron.I)

ka⸗ (prep.ptc.).:. *såar* (v.Z), (lex.int.phr.) 'to free from', 'to extract from'

ka⸗ (prep.ptc.) component of the above lex.int.phr.

såar (v.Z) component of the above lex.int.phr.; *saarin* (neg.pres.-past gen.); note that outside this lex.int.phr. this verb means 'to put [something] on top of [something else]'

ICC = !N5^C! *båa* *aan⸗* V2^C
    N5 = *cid*
    V2 = *saarin*

/15/ *Håadalkii duulåan Khadar hǫleelin.*

'[Even] Khadar does not recover words which have flown [away].' A modern poetic version of the proverb *Wåx tǫgåy Khadar må haleelô* '[Even] Khadar does not recover things which have passed.'

håadalkii duulåan = *håadalkii duulåy* + *båa* + *aan⸗*

håadalkii duulåy (nom.cl./smp.stg., clo.cfg.) 'the words which have flown [away]'

håadalkii (nom.aggr.I/intg.stg., cct.cfg.) = *håadal* + *kii*

håadal (n.m.) 'speech','words'

kii (def.art.rem.m.); - - - (form A)

dûul (v.Z) 'to fly'; *duulåy* (3sg.m.past gen.cvg.A)

bãa (ind.)

aan⸴ (neg.ptc.)

Khãdar (n.m.) the name of a saintly person who according to Islamic traditions has
    been alive since the time of Moses; he is believed to come to people's aid even
    in very difficult situations, (for further information see HA 74: 26-27); *Khadar*
    (smp.stg., ope.cfg., case B)

halèel (v.Z) 'to recover', 'to find something that was lost'; *ḥaleelín* (neg.pres.-past
    gen.)

ICC = ⸴N1⸴ *bãa aan*⸴ N2^C V2^C
    N1 = *hãdalkíi duulãy*
    N2 = *Khadar*
    V2 = *ḥaleelín*

/16/ *Nín is ḟaanshay waa rí is nuugtãy.*

'A man who has praised himself is [like] a goat which has sucked herself.'   Proverb.
This proverb is used either to censure boasting or to provide an excuse for one's
refusal to answer questions about one's achievements.

nín is ḟaanshay (nom.cl./smp.stg., ope.cfg., case B)

nín (n.m.) 'a man'; - - - (intg.stg., cct.cfg.)

is (rec.pron.) 'self', 'oneself'

ḟãani (v.IN) 'to praise'; *ḟaanshay* or *ḟaanshey* = *ḟaaniyay* or *ḟaaniyey* (3sg.m.past gen.
    cvg.B)

waa⸴ (ind.); *waa* (pos.var.)

rí is nuugtãy (nom.cl./smp.stg., neu.cfg.)

rí (n.f.) 'a goat'; - - - (intg.stg., cct.cfg.)

is (rec.pron.) 'self', 'oneself'

nuug (v.Z) 'to suck'; *nuugtãy* or *nuugtéy* (3sg.f.past gen.cvg.A)

ICC = *waa*⸴ ⸴N8⸴
    N8 = *rí is nuugtãy*

/17/ *Wãa ayŏ?*

'Who is it?'   AL 67: 7. A character in the play has an unexpected encounter with a
man he does not know and, in an aside, he asks a friend for information.

waa⸴ (ind.); *wãa* (pos.var.)

ayŏ (inter.w.V/smp.stg., neu.cfg.)

ICC = *waa*⸴ ⸴N8⸴
    N8 = *ayŏ*

/18/ *Waar rèeryahaw ma nabãd bãa?*

'Listen, o head of the family, is it peace?' AL 67: 3. These are the first words of
a newcomer upon his arrival at a nomadic settlement and are addressed to the head
of the family in the play.

waaʔ (r.i.) a word used for attracting the attention of a man or men, translated here as 'listen'; *waaʔ* (pos.var.)

* řeeryahaw = řeeʔ + yahawʔ*

řeeʔ (n.m.) 'a family', 'a settlement inhabited by members of one family', 'the head of such a settlement'

-yahawʔ or *-yohowʔ*, a vocative suffix used with masculine nouns

maʔ (ind.)

nabâd (n.f.) 'peace'; - - - (smp.stg. clo.cfg.)

bàa (ind.)

ma nabâd bàa, note that this is a conventional form of greeting

ICC = *maʔ* ¦N9¦ *bàa*
      N9 = *nabâd*

/19/   *Waa ín mârka horê naadiyâda lôo helaa mâamul wanaagsân.*

'It is necessary that one should first get good management for the clubs.' JA 74: 1 August, 3. From an article which stresses the necessity of various improvements in the organization and training programmes of football clubs in Somalia.

waaʔ (ind.); *waa* (pos.var.)

ín.......wanaagsân (para-nom.cl.I/smp.stg., neu.cfg.) 'that one should first get good management for the clubs'

ín (decl.ptc.) 'that'

mârka horê (nom.cl.I/intg.stg., ope.cfg., case A) 'first', lit. '[at] the time which is first'

mârka (nom.aggr.I/intg.stg., cct.cfg.) = *mâr + ka*

mâr (n.m.) 'time', 'point in time'

ka (def.art.gen.m.); - - - (form A)

horê (attr.) 'which is first'; - - - (form A)

naadiyâda (nom.aggr.I/intg.stg., ope.cfg., case A) = *naadiyŏ + ta*

naadĭ (n.m.) 'a club'; *naadiyŏ* (n.f.plur.)

ta (def.art.gen.f.); - - - (form A)

lôo = la + uʔ

la (impers.pron.)

uʔ (prep.ptc.) 'for'

hêl (v.Z) 'to find', 'to get', *helaa* (pres.gen.dvg.B); note that when the para-nom.cl.I refers to necessity, obligation, wish or intention and its verbal form belongs to the pres.gen.dvg. paradigm there is a tendency to use forms B rather than forms A.

mâamul wanaagsân (nom.cl/intg.stg., ope.cfg., case A) lit. 'management which is good'

mâamul (n.m.) 'management'; - - - (intg.stg.,cct.cfg.)

wanaagsân (v.SAN†) 'to be good'; - - - (pres.cvg.A)

ICC = *waaʔ* ¦N8¦
      N8 = *ín.......wanaagsân*

/20/ *Wallāahi wăx sų̆ṣurôobi kară wḛeyê.*

'By God, it is something that is possible.' HA 66: 3. This is a comment made by the hero of the play when he hears his friend's advice on how to silence a watch dog by giving it a camel's knee-cap bone to chew. The hero is planning an elopement and his prospective bride lives in a well-guarded house.

Wǫllāahi (r.i.) 'by God'; an interjection borrowed from Arabic

wăx sų̆ṣurôobi kară (nom.cl./smp.stg., neu.cfg.) lit. 'a thing which can become possible'

wăx (n.m.) 'a thing', 'things'; *wăx* (intg.stg., cct.cfg.)

sų̆ṣurŏw (v.OOB) 'to become possible'; *sų̆ṣurôobi* (inf.dep.)

kăr (v.Z) an auxiliary verb the meaning of which corresponds to 'can' or 'to be able to' in English; *kară* (3sg.m.pres.gen.cvg.A)

wḛeyê (ind.)

ICC = ⌐Nll⌐ *wḛeyê*
    Nll = *wăx sų̆ṣurôobi kară*

Wǫllāahi.......wḛeyê, note that there is no explicit subject in this sentence. If it were present it would occur either before N11 or after the ind.

/21/ *Sabăbtu wăxa wḛeyê in aannu dugsiyăda kŭ barannô manhajyŏ shisheeyê.*

'The cause [of it] is that in [our] schools we have foreign programmes.' Lit. 'The cause is that in the schools we learn programmes of foreigners.' JA 74: 1 June 2. From an article which exhorts authors to write educational books adapted to the needs of the country. The article deplores the neglect of the study of Somali history and geography and blames it on the school programmes brought from abroad.

sabăbtu (nom.aggr.I/smp.stg., ope.cfg., case B) = *sabăb* + *tu*

sabăb (n.f.) 'cause'

ta (def.art.gen.f.); *tu* (form B)

wăxa (ind.)

wḛeyê (ind.)

in.......shisheeyê (para-nom.cl.I/smp.stg., neu.cfg.) 'that in the schools we learn programmes of foreigners'

in aannu or, optionally, *inaannu*; both ways of writing this sequence are acceptable in the Somali orthography

in (decl.ptc.) 'that'

aannu (1pl.excl.subj.pron.)

dugsiyăda (nom.aggr.I/intg.stg., ope.cfg., case A) = *dugsiyŏ* + *ta*

dŭgsi (n.m.) 'a school'; *dugsiyŏ* (n.f.plur.)

ta (def.art.gen.m.); - - - (form A)

ku⌐ (prep.ptc.) 'in'; *kŭ* (pos.var.)

barô (v.AN) 'to learn'; *barannô* (pres.gen.dvg.A)

manhajyŏ shisheeyê (nom.cl.I/intg.stg., ope.cfg., case A) 'programmes of foreigners'

mănhaj (n.m.) 'programme', 'curriculum', 'method'; *manhajyŏ* (n.f.pl.); *manhajyŏ* (intg. stg., cct.cfg.)

shishêeye (n.m.) 'a foreigner', 'foreigners'; *shisheeyê* (sub.gnt.stg., ope.cfg., case A)

ICC = wáxa wg̃eeyḗ !N7!
    N7 = ín.......shisheeyḗ

/22/ Ma fílaysaa ín barnáamajkáa cusubi sídaad ugú talá gashg̃en sánnadkáas kú dhammaadô?

'Are you hoping that the new programme will finish in that year as you have planned?' JA 74: 22 June, 3. A question addressed to the Secretary for Education in a press interview about the new programme for mass literacy and fundamental education in the rural areas for the school year 1974-75.

ma﹗ (ind.); ma (pos.var.)

fíl (v.Z) 'to hope', 'to expect'; fílaysaa or fíleysaa (2sg.pres.cnt.ext.)

ín.......dhammaadô (para-nom.cl.I/smp.stg., ope.cfg., case A) 'that the new programme will finish in that year as you have planned'

ín (decl.ptc.) 'that'

barnáamajkáa cusubi (nom.cl./intg.stg., ope.cfg., case B) lit. 'that programme which is new'

barnáamajkáa (nom.aggr.I/intg.stg., cct.cfg.) = barnáamaj + káa

barnáamaj (n.m.) 'programme'

káa or káas (dem.m.) 'that'

cusúb (v.Z†) 'to be new'; cusubi (pres.cvg.B)

sídaad.......gashg̃en (nom.cl./intg.stg., ope.cfg., case A) lit. 'in the way in which you have planned it'

sídaad = sída aad

sída (nom.aggr.I/intg.stg., cct.cfg.) = sí + ta

sí (n.f.) 'way', 'manner'

ta (def.art.gen.f.); - - - (form A)

aad (2pl.subj.pron.)

ugú = u﹗ + ku﹗

u﹗ (prep.ptc.) 'in', 'according to'; this prep.ptc. refers to sída 'the way'

ku﹗ (prep.ptc.) component of the lex.int.phr. given below; in other contexts this prep. ptc. usually means 'in', 'with', or 'by means of'

ku﹗ (prep.ptc.).:. tálo (n.f.):: gál (v.Z), (lex.int.phr.) 'to plan'

ku﹗, see above

tálo (n.f.) component of the lex.int.phr. given above; talô or talá (intg.stg., ope.cfg., case A); note that in other contexts this n. means 'advice', 'considered opinion', 'sound judgement'

gál (v.Z) component of the above lex.int.phr.; gashg̃en (2pl.past gen.dvg.A); note that this v. in other contexts means 'to enter'

sánnadkáas (nom.aggr.I/intg.stg., ope.cfg., case A) = sánnad + káas

sánnad (n.m.) 'year'

káas (dem.m.) 'that'; - - - (form A)

ku﹗ (prep.ptc.) 'in'; kú (pos.var.)

dhammáw or dhammôw (v.AAN) 'to finish' (intrans.); dhammaadô (3sg.m.pres.gen.dvg.A)

ICC = ma﹗ !V1!
    V1 = fílaysaa

/23/ Maad ʼii shĕegtid ʼinaadeer yáad caashaqday?

'Cousin, will you tell me [please] - whom have you fallen in love with? HA 66: 1.
These words are addressed by the heroine of the play to a man who wants to marry her.
Instead of declaring his love directly he tells her that he has fallen in love but
without saying with whom.

> maad ʼii shĕegtid 'will you tell me [please]?'; this is a rhetorical question which im-
> plies suggestion and encouragement; an idiomatic English equivalent of this
> question, which is positive in Somali, would be 'Why don't you tell me?'

maad = ma⟨ + aad

ma⟨ (ind.)

aad (2sg.subj.pron.)

ʼii = i + u⟨

i (1sg.obj.pron.I)

u⟨ (prep.ptc.) 'to'

shèeg (v.Z) 'to tell', 'to report'; shĕegtid (2sg.rhet.)

> ʼinaadeer or ʼina'adĕer (n.m.) 'cousin', 'son of paternal uncle', also used as a term of
> familiar address to persons who are not one's kinsmen; ʼinaadeer 'o cousin.'; note
> that all nouns when they occur as forms of address but have no special vocative
> suffix, have the following accentual pattern: Accentual Unit 1 or 2 on the first
> or the only syllable and Accentual Unit 3 on all the remaining syllables, if any.
> Unit 1 occurs when the first syllable is short, and Unit 2 when it is long. Note
> that forms of direct address were not included in AN 64a but this could be
> remedied by referring to nouns in the above contexts as being in the vocative
> case (case C) in the ope.cfg.

yaad = yaa⟨ + aad

> yaa⟨ (inter.w.IV) 'who?', 'whom?'; note that in sentences containing yaa⟨ the verbal
> forms are the same as in those ICCs in which a masculine singular noun is empha-
> sized and is followed by the ind. bàa.

cáashaq (v.Z) 'to fall in love with'; caashaqday (2sg.past gen.ext.)

ICC = ma⟨ !N4⟨
      V4 = shĕegtid

Note that this example consists of two independent sentences. The first of them,
maad.......ʼinaadeer, contains the ICC given above. The second, yáad caashaqday, has no
ind., since it contains yaa⟨ (inter.w.IV), see Section X.

/24/ Dhuumashá dhábarku muuqdaa dhuumashá má ahá.

'Hiding [in which one's] back is visible is not [real] hiding.' Proverb. This proverb
is used when referring to a clumsy concealment of facts or inept lying on someone's
part when the truth is obvious to everyone.

> dhuumashá.......muuqdaa (nom.cl./smp.stg., ope.cfg., case B) lit. 'hiding in which the
> back is visible'

> dhuumásho (n.f.) 'hiding'; dhuumashó (intg.stg., cct.cfg.); dhuumashá is a junction form
> which occurs when another word follows immediately without a pause intervening (see
> AN 64a: 110-111 and MU 56: 18-20)

dhábarku (nom.aggr.I/intg.stg., ope.cfg., case B) = dhábar + ku

dhábar (n.m.) 'back' (part of the body)

ka (def.art.gen.m.); *ku* (form B)

muuqó (v.AN) 'to be visible', 'to appear'; *muuqdaa* (3sg.m.pres.gen.dvg.B)

dhuumásho (n.f.) 'hiding'; *dhuumashó* (smp.stg., ope.cfg., case A); *dhuumashá*, a junction form

ma⸴ (ind.); *má* (pos.var.)

yąhay (v.STR) 'to be', 'to belong to'; *ahá* (neg.pres.)

ICC = *ma⸴* !N5!
　　V5 = *ahá*

/25/　*Wánkii sow adígu iga máad qaadín?*

'Have you not taken the ram from me?' AL 67: 6. These words are addressed by the country wife in the play to her husband. She imagines that it was her husband who took away the ram and not the thief. She expects her husband to reassure her in this belief.

wánkii (nom.aggr.I/smp.stg., ope.cfg., case A) = *wán* + *kii*

wán (n.m.) 'a ram', 'a castrated ram'

kii (def.art.rem.m.); - - - (form A)

sow⸴ or *soo⸴* (ind.); *sow* (pos.var.)

adígu (nom.aggr.I/smp.stg., ope.cfg., case B) = *adi⸴* + *ku*

adi⸴ (2sg.subs.pron.)

ka (def.art.gen.m.); *ku* (form B)

iga = *i* + *ka⸴*

i (1sg.obj.pron.I)

ka⸴ (prep.ptc.) 'from'

máad = *ma⸴* + *aad*

ma⸴ (ind.)

aad (2sg.subj.pron.)

qáad (v.Z) 'to take'; *qaadín* (neg.pres.-past gen.)

ICC = *sow⸴ ma⸴* !N5!
　　V5 = *qaadín*

/26/　*Miyáad kaxáynaysaa?*

'Are you taking them away?' AL 67: 12. A member of a vigilante group in the play, who arrested some thieves, remonstrates with one of the policemen who wants to take them away to the police station and charge them according to the law.

miyáad = *miyáa* + *aad*

miyáa (ind.)

aad (2sg.subj.pron.)

kaxée or *kexée* (v.AYN) 'to drive', 'to conduct'; here: 'to take away'; *kaxáynaysaa* or *kexéyneysaa* (2sg.pres.cnt.ext.)

ICC = *miyằa* N2^C ⋮V1^C⋮
    N2 = *aad*
    V1 = *kaxấynaysaa*

/27/ *Nĭn Islằam ẵh miyắanad ahằyn?*

'Are you not a Muslim man?' AL 67: 3. This question is asked by a character in the play as he attempts to dissuade another character from breaking his promise.

nĭn Islằam ẵh (nom.cl./smp.stg., ope.cfg., case A) lit. 'a man who is [a member of] the Islamic Community' or 'a man who belongs to the Islamic Community'

nĭn (n.m.) 'man', - - - (intg.stg., cct.cfg.)

Islằam or *Islằan* (n.m.) 'Islam', 'the Islamic Community', - - - (intg.stg., ope.cfg., case A)

yặhay (v.STR) 'to be', 'to belong to'; *ẵh* (pres.cvg.A); note that the final *h* in *ẵh* is not pronounced in this context but is written here in conformity with the usage of Somali national orthography

miyắanad = *miyằa* + *aan⸍* + *aad*

miyằa (ind.)

aan⸍ (neg.ptc.)

aad (2sg.subj.pron.)

yặhay (v.STR) 'to be', 'to belong'; *ahằyn* (neg.pres.-past)

ICC = *miyằa aan⸍* N2^C ⋮V2^C⋮
    N2 = *aad*
    V2 = *ahằyn*

/28/ *Carrừurtu mẫrkaad dhacdô wặy qososhaa, mẫrkay dhacdắna wặy ǫydaa.*

'Children laugh when you fall, but they cry when they fall.' Proverb. This proverb refers not only to the behaviour of children but also comparable attitudes in some adults.

carrừurtu (nom.aggr.I/smp.stg., ope.cfg., case B) = *carrừur* + *tu*

carrừur (n.f.coll.) 'children'

ta (def.art.gen.f.); *tu* (form B)

mẫrkaad dhacdô (nom.cl./smp.stg., ope.cfg., case A) lit. '[at] the time [in] which you fall'

mẫrkaad = *mẫrka aad*

mẫrka (nom.aggr.I/intg.stg., cct.cfg.) = *mẫr* + *ka*

mẫr (n.m.) 'time', 'point in time'

ka (def.art.gen.m.); - - - (form A)

aad (2sg.subj.pron.)

dhẫc (v.Z) 'to fall'; *dhacdô* (2sg.pres.gen.dvg.A)

wặy = *waa⸍* + *ay*

waa⸍ (ind.)

ay (3sg.f.subj.pron.)

qôsol (v.Z) 'to laugh'; *qososhaa* (3sg.f.pres.gen.ext.)

mȧrkay dhacdȧna = mȧrkay dhacdȯ na⌐

mȧrkay dhacdȯ (nom.cl/smp.stg., ope.cfg., case A) lit. '[at] the time [in] which they fall'

mȧrka (nom.aggr.I/intg.stg., cct.cfg.) = *mȧr + ka*

mȧr (n.m.) 'time', 'point in time'

ka (def.art.gen.m.); - - - (form A)

ay (3sg.f.subj.pron.)

dhȧc (v.Z) 'to fall'; *dhacdȯ* (3sg.f.pres.gen.dvg.A)

na⌐ (conj.) 'and', 'but'

wȧy = waa⌐ + ay

waa⌐ (ind.)

ay (3sg.f.subj.pron.)

o̧y (v.Z) 'to cry'; *o̧ydaa* (3sg.f.pres.gen.ext.)

Carrȧurtu.......o̧ydaa, note that this example consists of two sentences linked by the conj. *na⌐*:

(1) *Carrȧurtu mȧrkaad dhacdȯ wȧy qososhaa.*

(2) *Mȧrkaad dhacdȧna wȧy o̧ydaa.*

ICC (1) = *waa⌐ !V1!*
     V1 = *qososhaa*

ICC (2) = *waa⌐ !V1!*
     V1 = *o̧ydaa*

/29/ *Waar bȩryȧhaba wȧu i ha̧yee wȧanad o̧gȇyne, cȧashaq bȧan ahay.*

'Listen, it has kept its hold on me all the time but you did not know about it; I am in love.' AL 66: 2. In this sentence a character in the play replies to a question put to him by his friend who is surprised to hear about his falling in love.

waar⌐ (r.i.) a word used for attracting the attention of a man or men, translated here as 'listen'; *waar* (pos.var.)

bȩryȧhaba, lit. 'all the times', = *bȩryȧha ba⌐*

bȩryȧha (nom.aggr.I/smp.stg., ope.cfg., case A) = *bȩryŏ + ka*

bȩri (n.m.) 'time', 'period of time'; *bȩryŏ* (n.m.pl.)

ka (def.art.gen.m.); - - - (form A)

ba⌐ (distr.ptc.) 'each', 'all'; *ba* (pos.var.)

wȧu = waa⌐ + uu

waa⌐ (ind.)

uu (3sg.m.subj.pron.), translated here by 'it'; the reference here is to the word *cȧashaq* (n.m.) 'love', mentioned earlier in the conversation

i (1sg.obj.pron.I)

ha̧yee = ha̧yay ee

hȧy (v.IN) 'to hold,' 'to keep one's hold on'; *ha̧yay* or *ha̧yey* (3sg.m.past gen.ext.)

ee⌐ or *e⌐* (conj.) 'and', 'but'

wáanad = *waa⸗* + *aan⸗* + *aad*

waa⸗ (ind.)

aan⸗ (neg.ptc.)

aad (2sg.subj.pron.)

ǫgèyne = *ǫgèyn e⸗*

ǫg (v.Z†) 'to know', 'to be aware of'; *ǫgèyn* or *ǫgàyn* (neg.pres.-past gen.)

e⸗ or *ee⸗* (conj.) 'and', 'but'

cáashaq (n.m.) 'love', 'a person who is in love', - - - (smp.stg., clo.cfg.).

bàan = *bàa* + *aan*

bàa (ind.)

aan (1sg.subj.pron.)

yǎhay (v.STR) 'to be', 'to belong to'; *ahay* (1sg.pres.ext.)

Waaʁ.......ahay, this example is composed of three sentences:

(1)   *waaʁ.......hǎyee*

(2)   *wáanad ǫgèyne*

(3)   *cáashaq bàan ahay*

ICC (1) = *waa⸗* !V1!
       V1 = *hǎyay*

ICC (2) = *waa⸗ aan⸗* N2^C !V2^C!
       N2 = *aad*
       V2 = *ǫgèyn*

ICC (3) = !N1! *bàa* N2^C V1^C
       N1 = *cáashaq*
       N2 = *aan*
       V1 = *ahay*

/30/   *Bal yaan dèʁisku inna máqlin oo soddóh xún lay mǫodine!*

'Let not the neighbours hear us and let not people imagine that I am a bad mother-in-law!' AL 66: 4. The woman in the play asks her daughter-in-law to speak less loudly and with less bitterness for fear of their being overheard. The daughter-in-law has come to complain about her husband's outrageous behaviour.

    bal (r.i.), this word is very difficult to translate; in most contexts it corresponds to 'now', 'now then' in English when these words are used expletively; here the nearest equivalent might be 'still', 'yet', but the word has been left out of the translation given above.

yaan⸗ (ind.)

dèʁisku (nom.aggr.I/smp.stg., ope.cfg., case B) = *dèʁis* + *ku*

dèʁis (n.m.) 'a neighbour', 'neighbours'

ka (def.art.gen.m.); *ku* (form B)

inna or *ina* (1pl.incl.obj.pron.I)

máqal (v.Z) 'to hear'; *máqlin* (neg.opt.); note that this verb has an alternating root:
    maqal-maql

oo⸗ (conj.) 'and'; *oo* (pos.var.)

soddôh xûn (nom.cl./smp.stg., ope.cfg., case A) lit. 'a mother-in-law who is bad'

soddôh (n.f.) 'mother-in-law', - - - (intg.stg., cct.cfg.)

xûn (v.Z†) 'to be bad'; - - - (pres.cvg.A)

ḷay = ḷa i

ḷa (impers.pron.) 'someone', 'one', 'people'

i (1sg.obj.pron.I)

mǫodine = mǫodin e

mǫod (v.Z) 'to mistake [someone or something] for', 'to imagine', 'to suppose'; *mǫodin* (neg.opt.)

e⸴ or *ee⸴* (conj.) 'and'; this conjunction is often added to neg.opt. forms without any specific meaning

Baḷ.......mǫodine, note that the whole sentence may be regarded as a conflation of two sentences:

(1) *Baḷ yaan dęrisku inna mâqḷine.* and

(2) *Yaan soddôh xûn ḷay mǫodine.*

```
ICC (1) = yaan⸴ N2ᶜ ⸴V7ᶜ⸴
          N2 = dęrisku
          V7 = mâqḷin
ICC (2) = yaan⸴ N2ᶜ ⸴V7ᶜ⸴
          N2 = ḷa
          V7 = mǫodin
```

/31/ *Intay caḷôoshu bûki ḷahâyd câgtu hâ bukto.*

'In circumstances when the stomach would become ill, let the foot be ill [instead].' Proverb. In Somali the stomach is spoken of as the seat of the emotions and this proverb suggests that when circumstances arise which could lead to enmity between people one should immediately try to bring about a reconciliation. Since in the nomadic interior mediation and arbitration usually involve travel, a peace-maker could easily develop 'ill', i.e. sore, feet.

intay.......ḷahâyd (nom.cl./smp.stg., ope.cfg., case A) '[in] circumstances when the stomach would become ill'; other interpretations are also possible: 'as long as the stomach might be ill' or 'instead of the stomach being ill'

intay = inta ay

inta (nom.aggr.I/intg.stg., cct.cfg.) = *in + ta*

in (n.f.) 'amount', 'period of time', 'circumstances'

ta (def.art.gen.f.); - - - (form A)

ay (3sg.f.subj.pron.)

caḷôoshu (nom.aggr.I/intg.stg., ope.cfg., case B) = *caḷôoḷ + tu*

caḷôoḷ (n.f.) 'stomach', 'belly'

ta (def.art.gen.f.); *tu* (form B)

bûg (v.Z) 'to be ill'; *bûki* (inf.dep.); note that this verb has an alternating root: *bug-buk*

ḷêh or *ḷe* (v.Z†) an auxiliary verb used here with the inf.dep. form *bûki* conveying the notion of conditionality; *ḷahâyd* (3sg.f.past gen.dvg.A) but note that this form of the auxiliary verb need not necessarily refer to the past

cãgtu (nom.aggr.I/smp.stg., ope.cfg., case B) = *cag + tu*

cãg (n.f.) 'foot'

ta (def.art.gen.f.); *tu* (form B)

ha⸴ (ind.); *hã* (pos.var.)

bũg (v.Z) 'to be ill'; *bukto* (3sg.f.optat.)

ICC = *ha⸴* !N8!
    V8 = *bukto*

/32/   *Ha ̃ii sõo noqõnnin!*

'Do not come back to me!' AL 67: 8. These words are addressed by the country thief in the play to the town thief who tried unsuccessfully to steal a ram from him.

ha⸴ (ind.); *ha* (pos.var.)

̃ii = i + u⸴

i (1sg.obj.pron.I)

u⸴ (prep.ptc.) 'to'

sõo (adv.ptc.).:. *noqõ* (v.ON), (lex.int.phr.) 'to come back'

sõo (adv.ptc.) component of the above lex.int.phr.; note that in most other contexts
        means 'towards [what is regarded by the speaker as the centre of attention]'

noqõ (v.ON) component of the above lex.int.phr.; note that by itself this verb means
        'to become'; *noqõnnin* (2sg.neg.imper.)

ICC = *ha⸴* !N9!
    V9 = *noqõnnin*

Section XIII

CLASSIFIED INDEX OF EXAMPLES USED IN SECTIONS VII AND XII

All the annotated examples used in this article are listed below. They are arranged according to the ICCs which occur in them and are divided into two columns headed by the figures VII and XII. These figures refer to the sections in which the examples are used, while the figures in the columns refer to the serial numbers of the examples.

	VII	XII
!N1! *bãa* N2^C V1^C	1, 2	1, 2, 29
ma⸴ !N3! *bãa* N2^C V1^C	3	3
wãxa N2^C V1^C !N4!	4	4, 12
ma⸴ *wãxa* N2^C V1^C !N4!	5	5
!N1! *bãa aan⸴* N2^C V2^C	6	6, 15
ma⸴ !N3! *bãa aan⸴* N2^C V2^C	7	

(Classified Index continued)

	VII	XII
wáxa aan⌐ N2^C V2^C !N4!	8	7, 8
!N5^C! bãa V3^C	9	6, 9, 10
ma⌐ !N6^C! bãa V3^C	10	11
!N6^C! míyãa V3^C	11	12
wáxa V3^C !N7^C!	12	13
!N5^C! bãa aan⌐ V2^C	13	14
ma⌐ !N6^C! bãa aan⌐ V2^C	14	
wáxa aan⌐ V2^C !N7^C!	15	
waa⌐ !N8!	16, 19	6, 16, 17, 19
ma⌐ !N9! bãa	17, 20	18
!N10! míyãa	18	
!N11! wẹeyẽ	21, 22	20
wáxa wẹeyẽ !N7!	23	21
ma⌐ !V1!	24	22
ma⌐ !V4!	25	23
ma⌐ !V5!	26	24
soo⌐ ma⌐ !V5!	27	25
míyãa N2^C !V1^C!	28	26
míyãa aan⌐ N2^C !V2^C!	29	27
soo⌐ míyãa aan⌐ N2^C !V2^C!	30	
soo⌐ !V6!	31	
waa⌐ !V1!	32	28
waa⌐ aan⌐ N2^C !V2^C!	33	29
yaan⌐ N2^C !V7^C!	34	30
ha⌐ !V8!	35	31
ha⌐ !V9!	36	33

Section XIV

REFERENCES

Throughout this article the works listed in this section are referred to by the first two letters of the author's name and the last two figures of the year of publication, e.g. AR 34 means Armstrong 1934. In the case of newspaper articles the day and month of the issue is given after the figures referring to the year. Figures which follow the types of entry described above refer to pages.

The names of Somali authors are entered in the list alphabetically, but starting with the first names, since no surnames are normally used in Somalia, hence Ali Sugule and not Sugule, Ali. When a Somali name is written in the form it had before the introduction of the national orthography, the orthographic version is given in brackets.

Items AL 66, AL 67 and HA 66 have not yet been published but their texts in typewritten form have been deposited in the Library of the School of Oriental and African Studies, University of London. Information concerning the authors of these plays and their other works can be found in the introduction to HA 74.

Item MU 56 contains fully annotated narratives, with English vocabularies; English translations of Texts 1, 8, 12, 13, 14, 18, 19, 21 and 23 of MU 56 are available in AN 64b.

Some readers may experience difficulties if they wish to obtain items AN 64a, GU 61 and MU 56, but these can be ordered from the Publications Officer, School of Oriental and African Studies, University of London, London WC1E 7HP.

Bibliographical references to Zholkovsky's works not mentioned here can be found in HA: 40 and ZH 71: 262-263.

Abraham, R.C. 1964. *Somali-English Dictionary*. London: University of London Press. [Pp. 258-332 contain an outline of Somali grammar.]

Ali Sugule (Cali Sugulle). 1966. *Kalahaab iyo kalahaad*. A play recorded during a stage performance and transcribed from tapes by Omar Au Nuh (Cumar Aw Nuux). Typescript. Mogadishu.

_____. 1967. *Tuug tuug ma chado*. A radio play recorded from a broadcast by Radio Mogadishu and transcribed from tapes by Omar Au Nuh (Cumar Aw Nuux). Typescript. Mogadishu.

Andrzejewski, B.W. 1954. "Some Problems of Somali Orthography," *Somaliland Journal* I:1.34-47.

_____. 1960. "Pronominal and Prepositional Particles in Northern Somali," *African Language Studies* I. 96-108.

_____. 1961. "Notes on the Substantive Pronouns in Somali," *African Language Studies* II. 80-99.

_____. 1964a. *Declensions of Somali Nouns*. London: School of Oriental and African Studies.

_____. 1964b. "Somali Stories," in *A Selection of African Prose: I. Traditional Oral Texts*, ed. W.H. Whiteley, Oxford: Clarendon Press. Pp.134-163.

_____. 1968. "Inflectional Characteristics of the So-Called 'Weak Verbs' in Somali," *African Language Studies* IX.1-51.

_____. 1969. "Some Observations on Hybrid Verbs in Somali," *African Language Studies* X.47-89.

_____. 1971. "The Rôle of Broadcasting in the Adaptation of the Somali Language to Modern Needs," in *Language Use and Social Change*, ed. W.H. Whiteley, London: Oxford University Press. Pp.262-273.

_____. 1974a (actually published in 1975). "Verbs with Vocalic Mutation in Somali and their Significance for Hamito-Semitic Comparative Studies," in *Hamito-Semitica: Proceedings of a Colloquium held by the Historical Section of the Linguistics Association (Great Britain) at the School of Oriental and African Studies on the 18th, 19th and 20th March 1970*, ed. J. and Th. Bynon. The Hague: Mouton, Janua Linguarum, Series Practica. Pp.361-376.

_____. 1974b. "The Introduction of a National Orthography for Somali," *African Language Studies* XV.199-203.

_____ and Lewis, I.M. 1964. *Somali Poetry: An Introduction*. Oxford: Clarendon Press.

_____ and Musa H.I. Galaal (Muuse X.I. Galaal). 1966. "The Art of the Verbal Message in Somali Society," in *Neue Afrikanistische Studien*, ed. Johannes Lukas. Hamburg: Hamburger Beiträge zur Afrika-Kunde, V. Pp.29-39.

Armstrong, Lilias E. 1934. "The Phonetic Structure of Somali," *Mitteilungen des Seminars für Orientalische Sprachen zu Berlin* XXXVII:III.116-161. [Reprinted in 1964 by Gregg Press, East Ridgewood, New Jersey.]

Axmed Cali. 1974. "Horumarinta afku waa xil ina wada saaran," *JA* 74: 21 January, 5.

Bell, CRV. 1953. *The Somali Language*. London: Longmans. [Reprinted in 1968 by Gregg International Publishers, Farnborough.]

Guthrie, Malcolm. 1961. *Bantu Sentence Structure*. London: School of Oriental and African Studies.

Hassan Sheikh Mumin (Xasan Sheekh Muumin). 1966. *Hubsiino hal baan siistay*. A radio play recorded from a broadcast by Radio Mogadishu and transcribed from tapes by Omar Au Nuh (Cumar Aw Nuux). Typescript. Mogadishu.

_____. 1974. *Leopard among the Women: Shabeelnaagood - A Somali Play*. Translated with an introduction by B.W. Andrzejewski. London: Oxford University Press.

Hetzron, Robert. 1965. "The Particle *bàa* in Northern Somali," *Journal of African Languages* 4:2.118-130.

_____. 1972. "Phonology in Syntax," *Journal of Linguistics* 8.251-265.

_____. 1974a. "An Archaism in the Cushitic Verbal Conjugation," in *IV Congresso Internazionale di Studi Etiopici (Roma, 10-15 aprile 1972)*, Rome: Accademia Nazionale dei Lincei, Problemi Attuali di Scienze e di Cultura, CCCLXXI, Quaderno N.191. II.275-281.

_____. 1974b. "The Presentative Movement," in *Word Order and Word Order Change*, ed. Charles Li [in press].

Jamhuuriyadda Dimoqraadiga ee Soomaaliya, Wasaaradda Warfaafinta iyo Hanuuninta Dadweynaha [= Somali Democratic Republic, Ministry of Information and National Guidance]. 1974. *Xiddigta Oktoobar*. [A daily newspaper, in progress; founded in 1973.]

Johnson, John William. 1969. "A Bibliography of the Somali Language and Literature," *African Language Review* 8. 279-297.

Moreno, Martino Mario. 1955. *Il Somalo della Somalia: Grammatica e Testi del Benadir, Darod e Dighil*. Rome: Istituto Poligrafico dello Stato.

Muuse Haaji Ismaa^Ciil Galaal (Muuse Xaaji Ismaaciil Galaal). 1956. *Hikmad Soomaali*. Edited with grammatical introduction and notes by B.W. Andrzejewski. London: Oxford University Press.

Zholkovsky, A.K. 1966. "Posledovatel'nosti Predglagol'nïx Častits v Yazïke Somali," in *Yazïki Afriki: Voprosï Strukturï, Istorii i Tipologii*, ed. B.A. Uspensky, Moscow: Izdatel'stvo "Nauka." Pp.143-166.

_____. 1971. *Sintaksis Somali: (Glubinnïe i Poverxnostnïe Strukturï)*. Moscow: Izdatel'stvo "Nauka."

FIRST NORTH-AMERICAN CONFERENCE ON SEMITIC LINGUISTICS

Santa Barbara, California
March 24-25, 1973

The first North-American Conference on Semitic Linguistics was organized by Robert Hetzron (University of California, Santa Barbara) with the cooperation of Giorgio Buccellati (University of California, Los Angeles) and Joseph L. Malone (Barnard College--Columbia University). The purpose of the Conference is to promote the interest of Semitists in the various modern currents of linguistics. The full list of the papers presented at the 1973 Conference is given below. Those papers which have been submitted and accepted for inclusion in *AAL*, like the present one, are being published within the framework of the journal.

A. Semitic and its Afroasiatic Cousins

1. Carleton T. Hodge (University of Indiana), *The Nominal Sentence in Semitic* (=AAL 2/4).
2. G. Janssens (University of Ghent, Belgium), *The Semitic Verbal System* (=AAL 2/4).
3. J. B. Callender (UCLA), *Afroasiatic Cases and the Formation of Ancient Egyptian Verbal Constructions with Possessive Suffixes* (forthcoming in *AAL*).
4. Russell G. Schuh (UCLA), *The Chadic Verbal System and its Afroasiatic Nature* (forthcoming in *AAL*).
5. Andrzej Zaborski (University of Cracow, Poland), *The Semitic External Plural in an Afroasiatic Perspective* (forthcoming in *AAL*).

B. Ancient Semitic Languages

6. Giorgio Buccellati (UCLA), *On the Akkadian "Attributive" Genitive* (=AAL 2/9).
7. Daniel Ronnie Cohen (Columbia University), *Subject and Object in Biblical Aramaic: A Functional Approach Based on Form-Content Analysis* (=AAL 2/1).
8. Richard Steiner (Touro College, N.Y.), *Evidence from a Conditioned Sound Change for Lateral ḍ in Pre-Aramaic.*
9. Stanislav Segert (UCLA), *Verbal Categories of Some Northwest Semitic Languages: A Didactical Approach* (=AAL 2/5).
10. Charles Krahmalkov (University of Michigan), *On the Noun with Heavy Suffixes in Punic.*

C. Hebrew

11. Joseph L. Malone (Barnard College--Columbia University), *Systematic vs. Autonomous Phonemics and the Hebrew Grapheme "dagesh"* (=AAL 2/7).
12. Allan D. Corré (University of Wisconsin, Milwaukee), *"Wāw" and "Digamma"* (=AAL 2/7).
13. Harvey Minkoff (Hunter College, N.Y.), *A Feature Analysis of the Development of Hebrew Cursive Scripts* (=AAL 1/7).
14. Raphael Nir (Hebrew University, Jerusalem), *The Survival of Obsolete Hebrew Words in Idiomatic Expressions* (=AAL 2/3).
15. Talmy Givón (UCLA), *On the Role of Perceptual Clues in Hebrew Relativization* (=AAL 2/9).
16. Alan C. Harris (UCLA), *The Relativization "which that is" in Israeli Hebrew.*

D. Arabic

17. Ariel A. Bloch (University of California, Berkeley), *Direct and Indirect Relative Clauses in Arabic.*
18. Frederic J. Cadora (Ohio State University), *Some Features of the Development of Telescoped Words in Arabic Dialects and the Status of Koiné II.*

E. Ethiopian

19. Gene B. Gragg (University of Chicago), *Morpheme Structure Conditions and Underlying Form in Amharic* (forthcoming in *AAL*).
20. C. Douglas Johnson (University of California, Santa Barbara), *Phonological Channels in Chaha* (=AAL 2/2).
21. Robert Hetzron (University of California, Santa Barbara), *The t-Converb in Western Gurage and the Role of Analogy in Historical Morphology* (=AAL 2/2).

F. Beyond Afroasiatic

22. Gilbert B. Davidowitz (New York), *Cognate Afroasiatic and Indoeuropean Affixes: Conjugational Person-Markers.*

ASSUR

ASSUR is meant to serve the needs of the specialized field which is closely identified with the study of Assyrian as a dialect of Akkadian and with the history of Assyria as a special aspect of Mesopotamian civilization, from early times down to the end of the Assyrian empire. Given the intensity of linguistic and historical exchanges with neighboring regions, it is clear that the study of Assyrian dialect and history cannot be carried on in isolation, without due consideration to influences deriving from contacts with other people. Hence, ASSUR will also accept articles which are not exclusively Assyrian in scope, as long as they are related to Assyria and useful for the study of its language and history.

Editors: K.-H. Deller, P. Garelli, C. Saporetti
(Address correspondence to Dr. C. Saporetti, Via Vasanello 20, Cassia, 00189 Roma, Italy)

Volume 1

Issue 1: S. Parpola, *The Alleged Middle/Neo-Assyrian Irregular Verb* *nass *and the Assyrian Sound Change* /š/ > /s/

Forms of the alleged irregular and defective verb *nass, reconstructed as occurring in Middle and Neo-Assyrian texts, are in fact to be understood as forms of the verb našû–and hence *nass is to be stricken from the dictionaries. The argumentation is based on five considerations. (1) Forms assigned to našû and *nass respectively are in perfect complementary distribution: missing forms of našû are covered by *nass and vice versa. (2) Semantically, both verbs are used in exactly the same function. (3) The paradigm is morphologically perfect in the sense that all forms of *nass conform to the paradigm of našû as known from the Old Assyrian period (in which no forms of *nass are attested). (4) There is firm evidence for the validity of the change /š/ > /s/ in the phonological system of Neo-Assyrian. (5) Writings with <sa> and <su> stand for phonemic /ssa/ and /ssu/.

Issue 2: C. Saporetti, *Some Considerations on the Stelae of Assur*

The publication of new texts has led to the identification of some of the eponyms mentioned in the steles of Assur. An analysis of the data results in a negative conclusion with regard to the possibility of arranging the steles in groups characterized by internal chronological coherence. The original sequence has been lost, and even within the same group there are steles dated to disparate periods, even if they are all Middle-Assyrian. Possibly, a subdivision may be suggested between the steles placed to the North, which may be rather late, and those placed to the South, which may be dated to the period of greatest power–but this differentiation might be accidental.

Issue 3: F. M. Fales, *Notes on Some Nineveh Horse Lists*

The article contains new documentary evidence on horses in Neo-Assyrian times, including the copies, transliterations and translations of three hitherto unpublished and four other texts from Nineveh. The discussion of the data provides an analysis of the internal structure and the nature of the texts. In one group, the horses are classified according to their color, sex and (possibly) age; these texts probably represent the preliminary listing of incoming animals, drawn up for internal use by the administrative unit of the palace in charge of horses. Another group consists of memoranda on specific quantities of horses, which are reports sent daily to the king by the same administrative unit, to provide an "ephemeral" (i.e. not destined to archival files) account of events.